*This book is sponsored by
the Allentown Downtown Improvement District Authority,
WAEB Radio, and
Air Products and Chemicals, Incorporated,
of Allentown, Pennsylvania*

Allentown

A Pictorial History

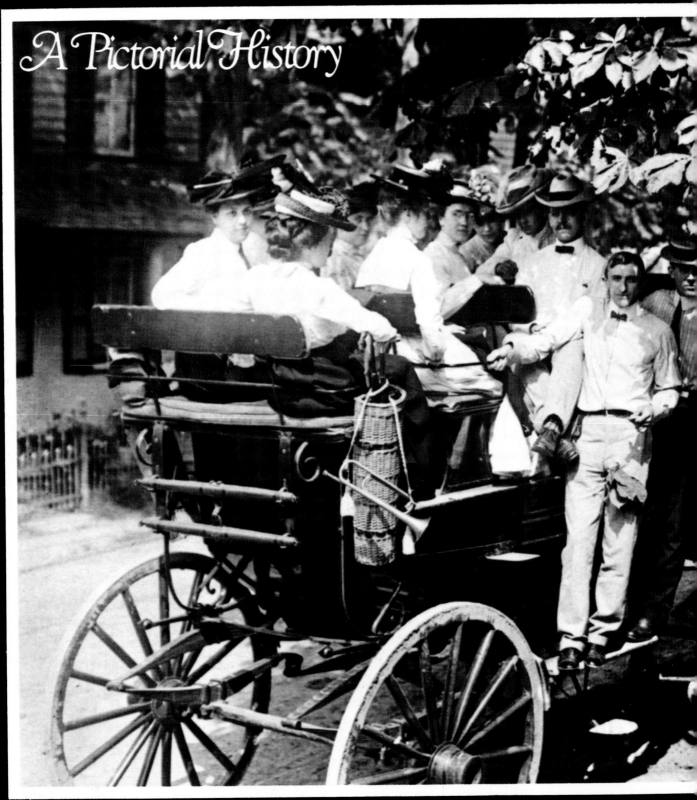

Ken Bloom and Marian Wolbers

Der Besht Blotz in der Welt

Als nuch dyer
Als nuch dyer
Hinkle, Hinkle
Lutheran Choir
Fire, Fire
We perspire
Lutheran Choir

The St. John's Lutheran Church Choir gathered in Allentown before heading to a picnic outing at Pleasant Corner on a sunny day in mid-July, 1901. *Courtesy of St. John's Lutheran Church*

Design by Jamie Backus Raynor
The Donning Company/Publishers
Norfolk/Virginia Beach

Debra Y. Quesnel, Project Director
Tracey Emmons-Schneider, Reprint Coordinator

Library of Congress Cataloging in Publication Data

Bloom, Ken, 1952–
  Allentown, a pictorial history.
  Includes index.
  1. Allentown (Pa.)—Description—Views. 2. Allentown (Pa.)—History—Pictorial
works. I. Wolbers, Marian, 1953– II. Title.
F159.A44B56   974.8'27   81-3128
ISBN 0-89865-131-X (pbk)   AACR2

Printed in the United States of America

Muhlenberg Lake at dusk, November,
1983. *Photograph by Ken Bloom*

To Zomi Louise

Contents

6:30 a.m. on "the Loop," mid-January of 1981. *Photograph by Ken Bloom*

CITY OF

ALLENTOWN

PENNSYLVANIA

18101

JOSEPH S. DADDONA

MAYOR

Historically, Allentown has always been a vibrant community, often in the forefront of new trends and developments. Allentown's economy has always been resilient and adaptable, as evidenced by its many phases and the various bases of support it has enjoyed through the Industrial Age. The changes forged by the evolving economic base of the city, combined with the continuing stability provided by the strong ethnic heritages of Allentown's people, tell an interesting American story. And the factor which I feel has, more than any other, accounted for the unique progress of our community is the continued willingness and ability of our people to work together toward survival and orderly growth.

As mayor of Allentown, I am filled with the overwhelming pride that comes with attainment of a high office—but with a deep sense of humility in the recognition of the awesome responsibility. I believe that each administration, regardless of the accomplishments of the past, inherits a challenging backlog of decisions to be made, problems to solve, projects to complete, programs to expand, and services to improve. Our city's crime-fighting and fire protection efforts, our parks and playgrounds, our street cleaning and water treatment, and our many other community services are not provided by and for Democrats, or by and for Republicans—they are by and for the people.

The role of the mayor, and the city government, is to identify and develop constructive trends and reinforce those trends with all the resources available to us. Governments at all levels—local, state, and federal—in recent years have been playing a less obtrusive and less partisan role in the physical, economic, social, and cultural development of cities. The large-scale urban renewal projects of the late 1960s and early 1970s are already relics. They have been replaced by projects which can be characterized as cooperative ventures among city governments, businesses, and property owners.

Most large and medium-sized cities in the northeastern United States have faced difficult times during the past ten years. We have witnessed the rapid growth of suburban America and the redirection of much of this country's wealth and population to Sun Belt communities. Allentown's diverse economy has given it some protection against these trends, but certainly the trends do affect the economic mix of businesses in Allentown. Since the mid-1970s, city government has become more aggressive in taking an active part in determining the direction of the city's economic development. Our efforts have stressed both helping existing businesses and bringing new businesses into the city, with the bottom line being the preservation and creation of more jobs for people.

Perhaps the most important economic trend for the future is the continued revitalization, strengthening, and expansion of the downtown central business district as a retail, commercial, service, and office center. Many city programs have focused on fostering this development, and a momentum is building which eventually will add a substantial number of jobs.

Ideally, more industrial plants would add to this broadening of the economic base. But unfortunately, cities that are as extensively built up as Allentown cannot easily accommodate substantial new industrial plant development. Virtually no space is left for such growth within the City of Allentown's borders. However, there is no doubt in my mind that rehabilitation of old existing buildings, while also attracting other types of productive businesses, is a significant part of the answer in maintaining a strong tax base. The vitality and diversity of activity available in a

1962-'63   1975-'76

center city are increasingly viewed as providing a more desirable setting than the sterile environment available in so many suburbs. We believe that the quality of life in Allentown will help bring corporate headquarters here.

This sort of development nicely complements the established industrial plant base provided by such staples of the Allentown economy as Mack Truck, Pennsylvania Power and Light, General Electric, Western Electric, Lehigh Structural Steel, and the numerous needle trade businesses.

Allentown is also a city of neighborhoods. As I mentioned, the trend is away from government imposing a heavy hand in how neighborhoods and their people live. The city has implemented programs which help neighborhoods and individuals to help themselves. To preserve and restore existing structures, and to preserve the individual social and cultural fabric of the neighborhoods of Allentown in as many ways as possible, we try to work cooperatively with neighborhood groups and with civic and citizen associations.

The city has done its best to encourage the resurgent interest in historic preservation as a means of revitalizing the housing stock of our center city neighborhoods. We have tailored our community development and housing programs to meet this objective, by sponsoring the Homesteading Program and the acquisition/rehabilitation and resale programs. Perhaps most important, we are administering two historic district ordinances which both encourage and control the exterior renovation in two neighborhoods of the city. Clearly, these types of cooperative ventures are the wave of the future.

I see Allentown as a community which will continue to evolve in the same imaginative and forward-thinking way that is its tradition. Further, I believe that Allentown will always retain a stability rooted in its multi-ethnic heritage, and that it is this heritage, combined with our optimism and positive determination, that can and will move Allentown dramatically forward in a way that will be an example for other cities. We can do these things because we are blessed with the kind of people who have the strength, the desire, and the resources to make it happen.

Joseph Daddona
Mayor of Allentown

Preface

As told by those who "remember when," stories about old Allentown take on special meaning. What has been remembered has endured in memory because of personalized impressions, like how it was to walk streets where peanut shells crackled under your feet, or how it was to see America as your new country as a child brought from Europe, or how it was to come from the coal regions to what seemed to be the big city. It seems surprising how the past passes from the public mind so easily when almost all of us can vividly remember being children in school, and how it felt, and what we remember seeing.

The job of writing history is one of restoring memory, even though many of the recounted tales refuse to fit nicely into formal time slots. It is as much a restoration of the human condition as fixing up a house in Old Allentown is a restoration of architecture. Many times a person would say at the end of an interview that he or she had not thought about the stories and mental landmarks for more than thirty, or even fifty years.

Each measured anecdote represents impressions and ideas formulated over years, and it always amazes us to think that a life story has been capsulized on ninety minutes of electronically etched plastic.

The focus of this book is its photographs. Although the images seem most obvious to the eye, mysteries hide in each photograph pulled from a box in the dusty attic. We do wish that someone would have written on the back what made each picture so precious to keep. The feeling is something like what happens when you handle a picture of a lovely young child with big bright flashing eyes full of anticipation for the future—except the picture is 100 years old.

What do 100 personal tales mean? What of the 105,000 people today in the city? What about their stories 100 years from today? How can we preserve some mark to represent their lives? About to unfold before you here is but a mere token intended to preserve what we could find to show of a community that has striven for more than 200 years to make something better for its children.

A wistful Millie Sweitzer Cosgrove surveys the Little Lehigh from the Eighth Street Bridge, circa 1920. *Courtesy of Ruth D'Aleo*

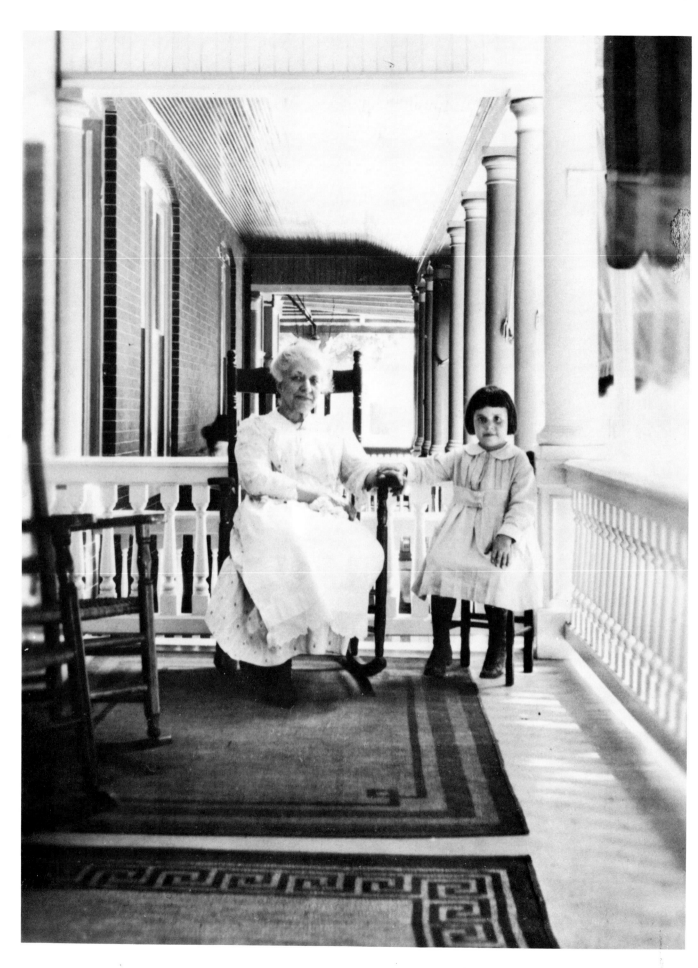

Introduction

The identity of this city called Allentown is revealed in the images throughout the following pages. It is in the dignified, determined faces of the Germans who first settled Mr. Allen's little town, as well as in the straight-forward gaze of a modern-day Syrian couple whose children were born in Allentown Hospital. It's in the mustachioed firemen parading at the turn of the century, and in storefronts draped with banners for the unveiling of the Soldiers and Sailors Monument. Allentonians boating on the canal, posing in oyster bars, walking the midway at the fair—all speak of a city that is many things to many people.

Allentown is a city of churches. In center city, it seems there is nearly one place of worship per block. It's a shopping town that has long attracted folks from all over the Lehigh Valley, including "coal crackers" from the northern coal regions, "steelers" from Bethlehem, and farmers from every direction. It's a residential city, a place with a personal flavor. Porch-sitting is a popular evening and weekend pastime from spring through fall, an activity that requires nothing more than enjoying the neighbors and cultivating a laid-back pulse.

Allentown is hometown. With a population of 105,000 and a wide diversity of businesses and industries, Allentown has found success, rooted in a tradition of hard work, home and family, and free enterprise.

The city's prosperity owes much to its location in the heart of the Lehigh Valley, where the Lehigh River and several creeks and streams cut through fertile farmland. At one time the Delaware Indians, or Lenni Lenape, enjoyed hunting game in the deep forests and fishing for trout in the Lehigh, but they lost claim to the area in the infamous Walking Purchase. According to a 1683 treaty with William Penn, white settlers were to have access to a land area determined by the distance a man could walk in three days. The actual measuring took place in 1737 upon the Indians' demand, since they were being pushed out. The walk was undertaken by three men known for speed and endurance on the trail, but their pace could hardly be referred to as even "swift walking." They ran for all they were worth, much to the deep resentment of the Indians. In the end, the boundaries owned by white men extended far beyond the Indians' expectations: from Wrightstown north to Blue Mountain, or approximately 500,000 acres.

In a little more than 150 years, the wilderness of scrub oak had become quite a different place: a city that was a nationally recognized producer of silk goods, cement, textiles, cigars, furniture, and iron. Its railroads gave direct access to the major centers of New York and Philadelphia. Immigrants from all over Europe had settled here, mostly on the advice of friends and family who had found jobs and built a good life for themselves.

"Dwell Here and Prosper" was the appealing slogan of the city in those days, and after another 100 years of growth and immigration that credo seems to have been prophetically well coined.

Ruth Taylor and her grandmother, Sara J. Mayne, porchsitting on North 6th Street, 1920. *Photograph by Mabel Mayne Taylor; courtesy of Liz and Ruth Taylor*

11

Allentown was mapped out in grid fashion, with forty-two blocks, between what are now Fourth and Tenth streets (east to west) and Liberty and Union streets (north to south). Judge William Allen gave credit to his family and friends in naming the streets, and his sphere of influence is revealed in the analysis. Allen Street (now Seventh Street), eighty feet in width including sidewalks, was to be the main north-to-south thoroughfare. It intersected a large public square with Hamilton Street, named for Allen's close friend and brother-in-law, James Hamilton. Turner Street honored Joseph Turner, Allen's business partner, from whom he acquired this tract of land; Chew Street was named for Benjamin Chew, who was a fellow judge on the Supreme Court. Sir Patrick Gordon was a former colonial governor; hence, Gordon Street.

Six of the streets Allen named after his children, with the four sons represented by the streets north, south, east, and west of the main Allen-Hamilton intersection: Andrew (now Linden Street), John (Walnut), William (Sixth), and James (Eighth), and the daughters flanking at Margaret (now Fifth) and Ann (Ninth). *Ink on paper, copied by Walter C. Livingston, 1824; courtesy of Historical Society of Pennsylvania*

William Allen (1704-80), founder of the city, was a man of wealth and influence who served as a judge and mayor of Philadelphia. *Courtesy of Lehigh County Historical Society*

Chapter One

Mr. Allen's Town
1762-1772

Colonial Governor James Hamilton was the brother of William Allen's wife, Margaret. He and James Penn visited Allen's lodge on the western bank of the Jordan Creek, hunting grouse and fishing for trout. The street bearing his name has always been the main center-city thoroughfare in Allentown. *Courtesy of Lehigh County Historical Society*

Allentown existed first on paper, its streets laid out in a neat north-to-south, east-to-west fashion. Two main thoroughfares intersected at a wide space set aside for a square—obviously earmarked as the town's marketing center. Building lots (over 750 of them) were all drawn up and ready for sale.

The site was perfect—a broad plateau at the confluence of three streams and overlooking the Lehigh River. The creeks were full of fish, the soil was good for farming. A major route, the King's Highway (Easton-Reading Road), passed through the town, providing access to Easton, Bethlehem, Reading, and beyond to Philadelphia and New York. All the dream town needed was people willing to step in and settle with their families, set up businesses, and make the place their home.

The town planner at work here was William Allen, an influential and respected judge from Philadelphia who had built himself a fishing and hunting lodge in the area and was fond of visiting whenever he could get away from the city. The son of an Irish merchant, young William schooled in England and returned to Philadelphia at the age of twenty-one to take over the business when his father died. He soon was on his way to a career in distinguished public service and at one point married Margaret Hamilton, daughter of Andrew Hamilton, who ranked as Speaker of the Assembly and Councilor for the Proprietors in the Colony.

In those days, land deals among men of high standing were fairly common (and useful in exchange for influence or goods or money), and so it was that William Allen bought the tract of land that was to become his town from Joseph Turner, his business partner, who had gotten it from Thomas Penn, who was deeded it from his father, William Penn, who got it from the Indians. Allen had his own reasons, political and otherwise, for wanting to develop a town much in the same manner as William Penn designed the very successful city of Philadelphia.

When it came to real estate, William Allen's timing was good. Although he had purchased the land in 1735, it was not until 1762 that he ordered his Northampton Town—known informally as Allen's Town—

13

surveyed, mapped out, and opened for settlement. By then, the backwoods had become dotted with the farming homesteads of more and more immigrants—most of them from various states in Germany, some from Switzerland, and some Huguenots and Quakers, too—who had responded to Pennsylvania's moral pledge as a hospitable territory free of religious persecution. The German Reformeds and Lutherans were the two most prominent groups, although there were some Mennonites as well, and they set up log churches in the wilderness in order to carry on their faiths. The churches doubled as schools for the children, and literacy was highly prized and encouraged.

Not surprisingly, these German-speaking immigrants, called Pennsylvania Germans or Pennsylvania Dutch (for *Deutsch*, or German), were the first to become citizens of Mr. Allen's new town. David Deshler, Abraham Rinker, Peter Rhoads, George Wolf, and their families all were early Allentonians who, along with the other "first citizens," brought with them their crafts and skills, learning, cultural tradition, and a strong sense of community, which shaped the essential character of the little colonial town.

It was an auspicious beginning, though the first years were a little rough. There was a drought throughout the summer of 1762, and in October 1763 Indians attacked settlers in nearby townships, creating widespread feelings of alarm and apprehension.

Growth was slow but steady. Tax assessment records show that there were thirteen taxables (only the names of men are listed) in Northampton Town after the first year and sixteen in 1763. By 1766 the assessment list had grown to thirty-eight, including a doctor, five "taylors," two shoemakers (one was also an innkeeper), two more innkeepers, a butcher, a locksmith, two bakers, a cooper (M. Cupper), four laborers, a mason, a potter, a carpenter, shopkeepers (who also ran the beer house and still house), three "joyners," and four "poor." The records of the following year, 1767, listed two women for the first time; both were widows. By 1772, not long before the Revolutionary War, the list was up to seventy-three, and Mr. Allen's little town continued to grow.

From 1767, William Allen's son James acted as town proprietor after his father deeded the land to him. He and his family stayed in Philadelphia most of the year, returning to Northampton only in the summertime to avoid exposure to malaria and the various diseases plaguing the port city of Philadelphia during the hot months. The summer retreat that he built here, called Trout Hall, became his year-round home and sanctuary during the troubled years of the Revolutionary War.

The Bogert cabin on the Little Lehigh Parkway was built in typical Germanic design sometime between 1739 and 1741. Restored, it stands near a covered bridge as a part of Allentown's extensive park system, where people can fish in the stream or picnic right next to the oldest home in the city. *Photograph by Ken Bloom, 1981*

James Allen (1742-78), third son of William Allen, became proprietor of the town when his father deeded him the land in 1767. A Philadelphia councilman, James brought his family to spend summers in the stone house known as Trout Hall, overlooking the Lehigh River. *Etching by Max Rosenthal; courtesy of Historical Society of Pennsylvania*

Trout Hall still stands at Fourth and Walnut streets, completely restored as a museum. It was built between 1768 and 1770 by James Allen, whose family used it originally as a summer retreat. In 1825 it was known as the Livingston mansion, and in 1848 the building became part of Allentown Seminary. Brick additions were built, and in 1864 it was made the Allentown Collegiate Institute and Military Academy; in 1868 the Lutherans bought it and founded Muhlenberg College there. Muhlenberg eventually moved to the west side of town, and when restoration was undertaken, the brick additions were removed. *Photograph by Ken Bloom, 1981*

Anne Penn Allen Greenleaf (1769-1851) was James and Elizabeth Allen's eldest of three daughters. Upon her father's death, she inherited a large portion of Allentown, and she lived here most of her life, devoting much energy to the development of the town. *Oil on canvas by Gilbert Stuart, circa 1795; courtesy of Allentown Art Museum*

Independence
1772-1811

The American Revolution

Allentown was destined to become vitally involved in the American Revolution. No fighting took place here, nor did famous military men hail from this busy little village of only about 300 people. But Allentown provided the "stuff" from which victory is made: equipment and supplies, food and clothing, strong leadership, and loyalty to the cause.

During the mid-1770s, Allentown grew increasingly prosperous—and political. The largely Pennsylvania German population, who were farmers, traders, and craftspeople, were not at all pleased with King George's taxation policies. Also, the small but industrious merchant class that had developed was not interested in being controlled from abroad, and their sentiments against the crown had a strong impact on the town's political pulse.

The church—in this case the Zion Reformed Church and its well-educated, influential minister, Reverend Abraham Blumer—played an important role at this time, for the church was the main social institution and center for exchange of ideas. Since it was based on volunteer principles rather than authority, the church fostered a sense of independence among members of the congregation, who saw themselves as Americans established in a community that no longer had ties with European rule. Several church-affiliated Pennsylvania Germans emerged as Revolutionary leaders: the Reverend Blumer himself; David Deshler, Peter Rhoads, and Peter Burkhalter, who were delegates to constitutional conventions; as well as Stephen Balliet; Peter Trexler, Sr., and Jr.; Peter Kohler; George Breinig; Henry Hagenbuch; George Graff; and others. As could be expected in a small community, several of these men were related to each other through marriage: Deshler's sister was married to Peter Burkhalter; Kohler's sisters married Peter Rhoads and George Graff; Burkhalter's daughter became Mrs. Stephen Balliet, and so forth.

By and by, the citizens' grievances toward the overbearing British turned to outright protest. Local committees organized first in 1774 and met in Easton with representatives from the county. The issue of

George Taylor (1716-81), an iron-master, was a prominent local leader who signed the Declaration of Independence in 1776 as a member of the Second Continental Congress. His summer mansion, built in 1768, still stands in Catasauqua, a few miles north of Allentown. *Oil on canvas by A. N. Lindenmuth, 1918; courtesy of Lehigh County Historical Society*

David Deshler and his wife, Susannah, are presumed to be the subjects of these oil paintings. Colonel David Deshler (1734-96), "first citizen of Allentown," was the town's first shopkeeper and owner of a gristmill and a sawmill. He was a patriot during the Revolutionary War and served as county representative when Pennsylvania ratified the Constitution in 1787. *Courtesy of Lehigh County Historical Society*

independence became a hot one in Allentown. With the presence of the aristocratic James Allen (town proprietor) and other crown-connected Northampton officials, Allentown looked Tory at first glance, but the German-speaking residents—who made up 90 percent of the town—supported the Revolution. So it was not long before a local militia began practicing maneuvers, and the town geared up for war.

By virtue of geography, economics, and a pro-freedom population, Allentown became a stronghold of the Revolution. In addition to supplying fresh produce from rich farmlands, Allentown was a manufacturing center for munitions, saddles, scabbards for bayonets, and shoes. A works for the repairing of arms and a Hessian prison were established in town.

James Allen was caught in the middle. In his diary (January 25, 1777 entry) he recorded:

> During October and November [1776] I remained at Trout Hall a calm spectator of the Civil War, but occasionally gave great offense to the violent Whigs [rebels] in Northampton by entertaining the regular officers, our prisoners, and was often threatened on that account.

Accordingly, when his brothers fled Philadelphia and sought protection from the British army, James found himself in a tenuous position as a Tory in Allentown. On December 19, 1776, at 7 a.m., according to his diary, a guard of soldiers came to Trout Hall and ordered him to appear before the Council of Safety in Philadelphia. What ultimately transpired in the trial was that Allen was allowed to stay in Allentown if he promised not to interfere with the local militia and local politics:

> In the afternoon they produced a certificate which they hoped I would not object to; wherein

they set forth, my brothers' departure, and the backwardness of the Militia as reasons for sending for me; that I had given them satisfaction respecting my prudent conduct; that my conduct did not appear unfriendly to the cause of Liberty, nor inconsistent of a gentleman; and I in return pledged my honor verbally not to say or do anything injurious to the present cause of America.

Things were generally quiet for the Allens thereafter except for one incident in which a company of hot-headed local militiamen attacked the family carriage with Mrs. Allen, daughter Peggy, and another child inside. The soldiers shoved bayonets into the carriage, broke the glass, and would have destroyed the chariot if Colonel David Deshler had not happened by. He stepped in quickly, reprimanding the soldiers and putting an end to the attack. Throughout the war, Deshler was to endear himself to the citizens as a just and dedicated leader. He was not only an officer but commissioner of purchases for the area. He offered his own property as shops for armorers and turned his tavern into a carriage factory, his lands into corrals for army horses.

Safe Harbor for the Liberty Bell

*I*n September 1777, as General Howe (British commander-in-chief) pushed General Washington's troops aside at Brandywine Creek and beseiged Philadelphia, the Liberty Bell (then the bell at the State House of Philadelphia) was secretly brought by wagon to Allentown, where it was hidden in the Zion Reformed Church along with the chimes from Philadelphia's Christ Church. This safekeeping prevented the British from melting down the bells for ammunition. James

David Deshler's gristmill was built on the Little Lehigh River. The drawing survives as a cabinet photograph taken by Lindenmuth Studio before the turn of the century. *Courtesy of Lehigh County Historical Society*

Allen probably knew about this clandestine act of patriotism, and his diary records the impact that Brandywine had on Allentown:

October 1, 1777: Since the battle of Brandywine many thousand Wagons passed by my door and are continually passing in great numbers. All the baggage of our army is at Bethlehem and here; and what with Hospitals and Artificers these little towns are filled. Every day some of the inhabitants of Philadelphia are coming up to settle here. The road from Easton to Reading, by my house, is now the most travelled in America.

James Allen died before the conflict was over, at the age of thirty-seven. His diary suggests that he was unhappy and frustrated at all the events taking place around him. He left most of his vast acreage to his son and three daughters and specified in his will that his three Negro slaves "shall be henceforth free and manumitted, I having ever been persuaded of the Injustice of Slavery."

From 1776 to 1780 the front was often nearby, so hospitals were set up for the sick and wounded soldiers that the Bethlehem facilities could no longer handle. The Zion Church expanded its functions again and turned into a temporary hospital.

Postwar Allentown

The end of the war brought an end to Tory privilege. Fortunes held in British notes were lost as the young nation developed its own currency. Those merchants imaginative enough to seize the opportunity and diversify their products and holdings—men like Peter Rhoads, David Deshler, and George Blank—

became men of influence. This was the beginning of the great diversity that characterizes mercantile Allentown to this day.

The town continued to grow slowly: in 1782 there were fifty-nine houses and over 100 cows. (Every family had a cow, but there were only eight horses in town.) By 1794 there were over ninety dwellings, two churches, and an academy. Reverend Blumer recorded that in 1785 there were thirty-five scholars in the school at the Zion Church. Ten years later, a second school existed opposite the church—an English school with its own schoolmaster, which remained there until at least 1825.

At Peter Rhoads' store in the 1780s and 1790s, items such as West Indian rum sold well in addition to the usual foodstuffs, fabrics, hardware, and almanacs. The ledgers show that twelve copies of *Robinson Crusoe*, the bestseller of the day, were also in stock.

Having burned its bridges with British trade, America as a whole suffered economic hardship for many years after the war, and the struggling federal government was pressed to raise revenue. When a tax was levied on property and homes (following rather too closely upon the divisive Alien and Sedition laws), it was met with violent resistance in Northampton and nearby Bucks County. With independence won at such cost—and initially spurred by tax issues—it seemed to the Pennsylvania Germans that they had traded one form of oppression for another.

An insurrection against the tax was led by John Fries of a neighboring township, and so the area became a proving ground for federal authority. Allentown tax assessors had to be appointed, since hardly anyone dared volunteer for the job, and there was so much controversy that President John Adams was forced to send in troops, who marched through the entire Quakertown-Reading-Allentown-Bethlehem area. Rebel leaders were charged with being traitors, imprisoned, and eventually pardoned, and the Fries

Rebellion (1798-99) was thus put down without bloodshed.

The blueprint for Allentown's future can be seen in events around this time, as Allentown came into its own. There was an attempt made in 1792, involving the Allens and Judge Peter Rhoads, to establish a separate county with Allentown as the county seat. In 1798 the Lehigh Navigation Company was formed, with Rhoads as president, with the intention of using the Lehigh River for passage. Both these projects proved unsuccessful in the short run, but they were farsighted attempts at establishing Allentown as a mercantile center and organizing a network for transportation and communication that would secure the town's economic strength.

Mr. and Mrs. Stephen Balliet had their portraits painted in 1787. Magdalena Burkhalter Balliet (1765-1805) was the daughter of Peter Burkhalter, a local Revolutionary leader. Her husband, Colonel Stephen Balliet (1753-1821), served during the Revolutionary War at the Battles of Brandywine and Germantown. As a politician, he served on the Supreme Executive Council of Pennsylvania as well as in the General Assembly. *Oil on canvas by S. Jennings, 1787; courtesy of Lehigh County Historical Society*

The Reverend Abraham Blumer was born in 1736 in Switzerland. Upon his arrival in America in 1771, he became pastor of the Zion Reformed Church, where he had an active ministry until 1801. Reverend Blumer was a patriot who assisted in hiding the Liberty Bell in his own church. *Courtesy of Zion Reformed United Church of Christ*

The first church in Allentown was a log cabin built in 1762. It housed both Reformed and Lutheran congregations. *Drawing courtesy of Lehigh County Historical Society*

The Zion Reformed congregation built a second church in front of the old church in 1773, and it was this building that concealed the Liberty Bell and other bells during the British occupation of Philadelphia (1777-78). *Woodcut from* Der Friedens-bothe *newspaper, June 1840; courtesy of Lehigh County Historical Society*

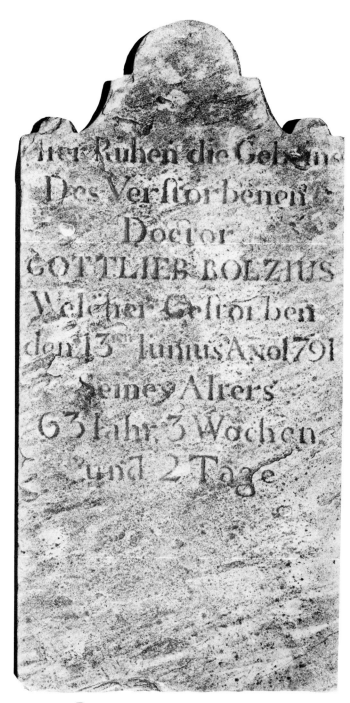

The memorial stone of Peter Rhoads (1737-1814) lists his many patriotic and political accomplishments. Rhoads was a man of influence: he was a tailor, owner of a general store, and a banker (though there was no bank as such) who extended credit and lent sums of money. During the war, his busy store was a central information agency of sorts, for all the news broke there. The gravestone is located in the Linden Street cemetery. *Photograph by Ken Bloom, 1981*

Doctor Gottlieb Bolzius, Allentown's first physician, came to the town in 1766. Upon his death in 1791 he left a generous legacy to the Lutheran congregation of St. Paul's Evangelical Church. His gravestone is in the Linden Street cemetery. *Photograph by Ken Bloom, 1981*

The Rhoads house was a fine stone structure, built in 1762. It stood for 200 years at 107 North Seventh Street until it was torn down in the 1960s. This photograph was taken in the 1890s. *Courtesy of David K. Bausch*

Perhaps owing to the absence of a photographic record, historical re-enactments of the Revolutionary War days are played out. Here ladies of the Christ Reformed Church, including the pastor's wife, Mrs. Lillian Sipple, pose in period costumes for the "First Washington Tea" around 1920. *Courtesy of Zion Reformed United Church of Christ*

Chapter Three

Allentown as a Borough 1811-1850

An important event in Allentown's history took place on March 18, 1811, when the Pennsylvania Assembly incorporated Northampton as a borough in an act signed by Governor Simon Snyder. Elections were then held at George Savitz's Compass and Square Hotel, and the borough's first officers included Peter Rhoads, who was burgess; also councilmen Graff, Martin, Miller, Keiper, and Nagle, whose names—of Swiss and German origin—clearly reflected the turnabout in power wrought during the Revolution.

One year later the assembly passed an act establishing Lehigh County as separate from Northampton County, in response to its growth in population. The borough officially remained Northampton in name, despite general disapproval, until 1838 when the name was formally changed to the more popular Allentown.

The earliest courts were held in George Savitz's hotel, a small two-story building that was also a post office and a tavern, but from 1817 on, a new courthouse built entirely in stone at Hamilton and Margaret (Fifth) streets was in operation. A jail erected four years before that proved useful until 1869, when the present, more imposing structure took its place.

In the early 1800s, with their county and borough established, the people set about organizing their commerce and industry. Great contrasts appeared as the agricultural town grew in population, developed an economy, and specialized its municipal services. Even in daily life, especially on the streets and in the alleys with pedestrians and bovines alike vying for space, rural informalities were forced to change. Town ordinances were passed prohibiting horned cattle from remaining on the streets at night from April to December, and horses were not to run at large any more (the fine was one dollar), nor were hogs (seventy-five cents) or geese (fifty cents). Wagons peddling water were the only means many people had of obtaining that essential commodity. The system was outdated, so in 1816 a water company—the Northampton Water Company—was organized. Initially progress was slow. Getting stock-

This chain suspension bridge, built between 1812 and 1814, was the first structure spanning the Lehigh River. The view looks west toward Allentown where, on the western entrance of the bridge, a large tollhouse stood. The flood of 1841 destroyed the bridge. *Oil on canvas, circa 1830, courtesy of Lehigh County Historical Society*

25

holders to support the venture was not easy, and twelve years passed before pipes were laid and a pumping works and reservoir were constructed. Silver Spring, which was near the Little Lehigh on the south side of town, was chosen to supply the borough's inhabitants.

Other projects were similarly organized. In July 1811 the town councilmen ordered "the Street Commissioner to provide fire ladders, one to be thirty feet long and the other to be twenty feet." But it was another seven years until, at the ever-popular meeting place, George Savitz's hotel, the Friendship Fire Company came into being. Then it was another two years before the town supplied the company with its first fire wagon, which had buckets and a hand pumper, at the handsome price of $524.

The growing community had to develop all its civic services from scratch. Not only were the townspeople in need of know-how, personnel, and facilities, but they had to depend on the distant existing markets of Philadelphia, New York, and Baltimore to satisfy the need for technology not available at home.

Access to other areas counted heavily. Stagecoaches were popular and readily available: a trip to Philadelphia cost about three dollars. Around town, it became obvious that a system of bridges would speed everyone along. Since the late 1700s there had been a bridge spanning the Jordan Creek at Union Street, but in 1837 a new, much more substantial bridge of stone was built there—a structure 800 feet long, 30 feet wide, and with eighteen arches. Over the Lehigh River, a 530-foot-long chain bridge was constructed in 1814, and the Lehigh Bridge Company was organized. The bridge had two suspended tracks for traffic going in either direction, and a four-dollar fine was imposed for trotting or galloping a horse over it.

Meanwhile, coal transporters were trying to work out a system of floating their cargo down the rivers on timber "arks" to their Philadelphia market. The marriage of the coal and navigation companies, the Lehigh Navigation Coal Company, led to the construction of the Lehigh Canal, which had fifty locks. In the early 1820s, some 2,200 tons of coal were shipped south, and by 1855 1,250,000 tons were sent. It was the heyday of the river industry. When the railroad was laid along the river in 1855, canal traffic began to drop steadily.

Business in the borough expanded, and so the first financial institution, the Northampton Bank, was established in 1814 on the northeast corner of the central square. Its president was Peter Rhoads, Jr., son of the

George Savitz became Allentown's first postmaster when a post office was set up in 1803 in his Compass and Square Hotel (later Hotel Allen). Before that, residents had to trek to Bethlehem for mail. Savitz's hotel also served as a bar, general meeting place, courthouse, and voting place. *Oil painting courtesy of Lehigh County Historical Society*

man who was truly the first banker with his general-store practices of extending credit and lending money. For twenty-eight years the bank was prosperous, as hotels and stores continued to spring up; by 1840 there were cabinetmakers and coppersmiths, shoemakers and brickmakers making their way in the town. Two floods, in 1839 and 1841, took their toll, with the latter wiping out the Hamilton Street Bridge.

The failure of the bank's credit in 1843 was a heavy blow. Then-president John Rice was blamed for wild speculation and bad management. Having lost their savings, the angry townspeople reacted. Rice was burned in effigy on the square after he had tried to leave town. Faced with overall financial collapse, business interests turned outside for investment and support in developing broader-based industry. From Philadelphia came money to purchase land and establish the Allentown Iron Works, which was to exploit local resources and labor. Yet the need for an extensive system of transportation for their products and coal supply made

the works dependent on regional cooperation. With the approval of the state legislature for a bond issue and with the sacrifice of valuable riverfront property in and near Allentown, the Delaware, Lehigh, Schuylkill, and Susquehanna Railroad Company was incorporated (eventually to become the Lehigh Valley Railroad Company).

The Ascension Day Fire

The flood of 1841 and the bank's fall ushered in what is referred to as the Disastrous Decade, from 1840 to 1850. The most devastating event by far, however, was the great fire of 1848, which swept the center of town, burning out the entire business section on Hamilton between Seventh and Eighth streets in a half hour, and leaving the finest part of the town in ashes.

It started at 3:30 in the afternoon on June 1, which was Ascension Day, in a tobacconist's stable between Hamilton and Linden. (Popular rumor blamed two disgruntled apprentices who felt they should have had the day off, but the true cause was never uncovered.)

The fire raged for three hours, fanned by a strong northwest breeze. Four fire companies fought the blaze with 400 feet of hose, two hand-pumper machines, and a bucket brigade, but with the wind and a shortage of water, it looked like the whole town would burn. In the end, thirty-five dwellings and forty-two barns and stables were lost, and property damage amounted to a crushing $200,000.

It was a slow recovery—nearly two years of hard work and hard times. As calamitous and horrible as it was, 850 families went to work rebuilding a modern town. A more efficient fire company was formed. Plans were laid for a stone reservoir holding 65,000 gallons of water. Donations came from as far as New Orleans. A new Hamilton Street was built, with some of the burnt lots selling for more money than they would have formerly with the buildings intact. Business prospects were excellent: the 1848 population of 3,700 jumped to 5,250 by 1854, just six years later. On a community level, deep and lasting friendships were formed during the time of crisis, as people were bound together in mutual support.

27

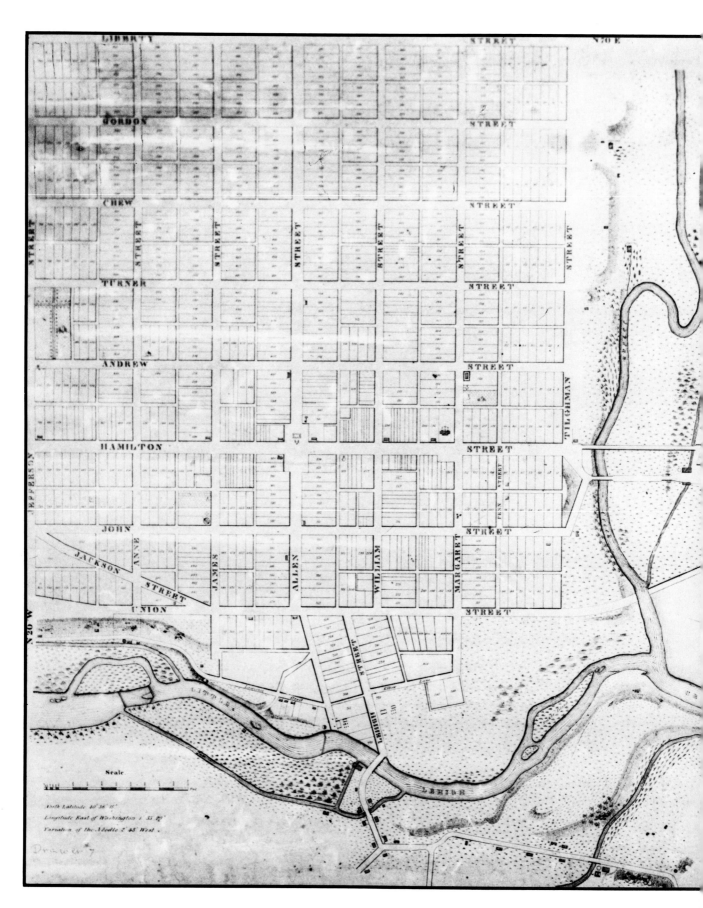

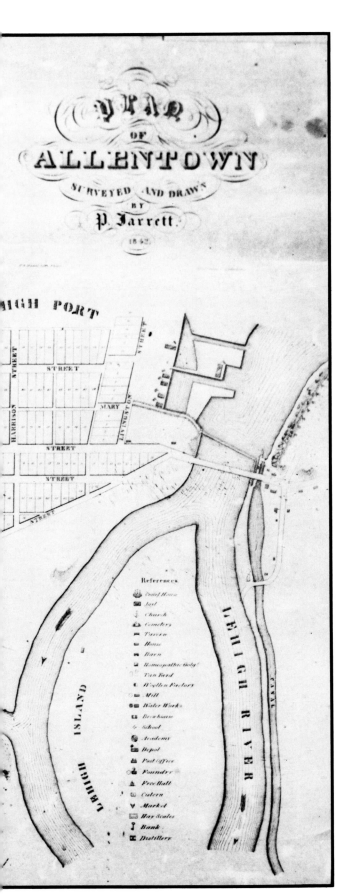

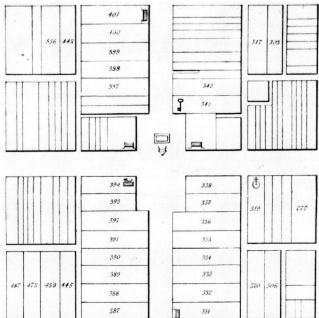

This map of Allentown, drawn in 1842, pinpoints spots of importance around the city. In the detail of Hamilton and Allen (Seventh Street), center square is marked with a bull's head, indicating a market, and a box for a hay scale; the circle with a cross is a church; the key represents a bank; the fish over a box is the post office; and the remaining four symbols stand for taverns. *Drawing by Phaon Jarrett, 1842; courtesy of Lehigh County Historical Society*

30

Allentown's Ascent 1850-1881

The earliest existing photograph of Allentown shows the southeast corner of center square with a covering of light snow in October 1862. *Photograph by S. W. Ochs, 1862; courtesy of Lehigh County Historical Society*

The decade leading up to the Civil War was one of great redevelopment and growth, and by the 1860s it had become evident that the business of Allentown *was* business. With the advent of the railroad, built by Asa Packer and extending from Mauch Chunk (Jim Thorpe) to Philadelphia, Baltimore, and other points, Allentown became a hub of shopping activity with its diversity of products and services. That particular character is very much the essence of Allentown today, as people from the outlying areas and neighboring counties make their shopping pilgrimage into the city.

In 1860 a family could be outfitted and an entire house and farm furnished during a shopping spree down Hamilton Street. There were yard goods and ready-made clothes, the best-known and still surviving outlet being Henry Leh's Lion Clothing Hall (now Leh's Department Store); there were milliners and tailors, jewelers and tinsmiths. Farm tools, hardware, and carriages were all for the buying. And, of course, a person's picture could be taken at a daguerreotypist's. Leh's advertised in an 1852 newspaper, "Daguerreotype likenesses taken in all weather for one dollar and warranted."

Another news account (*Lehigh Register*) of the times alerted shoppers that the merchants of the borough had agreed to close their stores earlier, at 8 p.m., except for Saturdays. As they put it, "The clerks will feel more energy after a little recreation in the evening." In general, an acceptance of more leisure in society seemed to be the trend, and there were various places to go to pursue pleasure. You could go to the Odd Fellows' Hall to take in a play put on by visiting acting troupes. A handwritten program of one evening's "Grand Entertainment" (March 28, 1867) included songs, piano and violin solos, comic drama, a situation comedy, lectures, and a scene from *Hamlet*. Parts one through four each ended in a tableau. Or a person could go on excursions to Helfrich's and Worman's springs or Adam's Island, or up to Big Rock on Lehigh Mountain for the view. (For young men that meant a view of the lovely ladies dressed in Sunday finery as well as the spectacular countryside.) One of the best times to go was on the first Sunday after the grain was cut, when thousands of shocks decorated the fields below. As for the care-

This is a town-and-country view of Allentown in 1853, fourteen years before the borough officially became a city. The core of Allentown was concentrated roughly between Fourth and Seventh streets, with such landmarks as Trout Hall, the dome of the courthouse, and the steeple of the Zion Reformed Church. *Lithograph by J. F. Louis, P. S. Duval and Company, Steamlith Press (Philadelphia); courtesy of Edith Mellner*

free life of a young man then, the *Lehigh Register* (January 15, 1852) tells the story of a daring young woman who dressed in man's clothes for a lark, to see what kind of fun she could have. He/she first went to a cotillion party at one of the hotels on Hamilton with cane in hand and a fat "segar" in her mouth. Several of the ladies were desperate to meet the man with such a sweet face and black ringlets, but alas, he/she went off to another popular spot to order up some oysters and drink beer. There her masquerade faded when a male acquaintance recognized her, and she left in a hurry, begging him not to tell her name to anyone.

The growth spurt Allentown experienced meant going from roughly 4,000 people in 1850, to 10,000 in 1859, to 14,000 in 1870. It meant that English was replacing German as the primary spoken language. Gas lamps lit the town, and there was a telegraph line. The number of churches increased. Several newspapers prospered. The stagecoach began to lose passengers as the railroad took over. Industry expanded. And community traditions that are still alive today became firmly established; namely, the bands, the annual fairs, the parades.

Bandleader Amos Ettinger organized about twenty-five local musicians in 1852, and the Allentown Band was born. A great deal of public enthusiasm and activity surrounded the band then (as now), and it and other bands occupy a unique position in Allentown's artistic life and the hearts of the people. During the Civil War many of the musicians became soldiers, and the band was dissolved until 1865.

The Great Allentown Fair had its beginnings as a community-interest project of the Lehigh County Agricultural Society when the group held the first Lehigh County Agricultural Fair during the height of the autumn harvest in 1852. The location was east of

Fourth Street between Walnut and Union. The following year saw the fair between Fifth and Sixth streets north of Liberty. Eight acres were permanently purchased in 1856 and used until 1889, when the present site was established in the west end on Chew Street. Like the Band, the fair was upset by the Civil War; in 1862 there was no event at all, as the fairgrounds were occupied by seven companies of the 176th Regiment, Pennsylvania Militia.

The Civil War: The First Defenders

"Let us hope that land is ahead, and that we shall soon be out of the sea of trouble, arising out of the Slave Discussion." So editorialized the *Lehigh Register* in April 1850. Alongside articles covering the gold rush to California it was becoming common to see mention of the antagonism growing between the North and the South.

Just prior to the war, in 1858, Allentown was feeling the depression that hit most of the nation. But once the war was on, Allentown was locked into business by the needs of the Union army and the profiteering that war brings. Manufacturers like Leh's supplied shoes. The Allentown Rolling Mills prospered as a forge and foundry, as did other iron-making enterprises. Trains connected Allentown with major centers—New York, Philadelphia, Harrisburg, Baltimore, Chicago. The combined sounds of the trains, the gristmills and sawmills, foundries and furnaces rang out a chorus of business and labor.

Community support for the Union was strong. Indeed, forty-eight men in the first regiment sent to defend Washington, D.C., came from Allentown. On April 15, 1861, President Lincoln issued a call for 75,000 men, but most immediately he needed two regiments since the capital was unprotected. Captain Thomas Yeager of the Allen Infantry offered his services and was instructed to bring his men to Harrisburg and on to Washington as soon as possible. He posted a volunteers' list on April 16, and at 4 p.m. the next day he and forty-eight men were walking down Hamilton Street to the train station amidst cheering crowds. So quickly were the citizens able to organize, they had collected all manner of clothing and necessaries, and had given these men, "the First Defenders," a fine send-off dinner at the Eagle Hotel.

Action came sooner than any of the new soldiers expected, though Captain Yeager had had some idea that their mission was going to be dangerous, if not suicidal. In crossing the Mason-Dixon Line, the companies (530 men in all) faced angry mobs outside Baltimore, particularly in the three-mile march from one depot to a train of boxcars bound for the capital. Rioters threw stones and bricks and insults, wielded

Dr. John C. Volker, a veterinarian, and his family lived in this house with gardens and a grape arbor on Seventh Street near Walnut. *Watercolor and ink by Frederick Wulff (Germany), 1855; courtesy of Lehigh County Historical Society*

clubs, and set fire to the bridge the soldiers' train was to pass over. Instructed by Yeager not to say a word or look around, the Allen Infantry got through to Washington with only a few men suffering serious injuries: two were made lame; one lost his teeth when struck with a brick; and another lost his hearing, also from a blow with a brick. It is said he struck back with the butt of his gun and tore off the attacker's ear.

Needless to say, further troops arriving by train were told not to dress like soldiers but like regular passengers, according to Yeager's account. Once the men reached Washington safely, they could don uniforms. The brave Captain Yeager was later made major of the Fifty-third Regiment, Pennsylvania Volunteer Infantry. But he was not to return home. He was killed in the Battle of Fair Oaks in June 1862.

An essay entitled "The Present War" by Moses A. Helfrich, dated March 19, 1863, gives us an idea of one boy's thoughts while a student at Allentown Collegiate Institute and Military Academy:

At present it is war; it is nearly two years that the war has commenced and we do not see an end of it yet. I suppose more than one hundred thousand people have shed their blood in this war, the cause of it I do not know. Some people say that Lincoln was the cause of the war [because] he would make the slaves free, [and] now they are free; but I suppose if [the Confederacy wishes to] wage war, they [the slaves] would not be free. But I say too, for my part, let those poor slaves be free, they are as good as we are. And yet, some say the slaves have no souls. That is not true: they are as good as we are. Who would like to be a slave?—that I would like to know. Why, nobody would like to be sold like a horse, and work only for food, they are only colored that's all. But I suppose the cause is that the [Southern] people were too headstrong. They would not follow the Constitution, and therefore they rebelled against our glorious Union. But I wish the war would soon come to an end, so that our stars and stripes could be unfurled and wave in every part of our Union which was so long united,...we thought that no nation could have risen against it....I wish that God would help to unite it again, so that peace would be restored.

—Courtesy of J. William Fritsch

Allentown Achieves City Status

As of March 1867 Allentown was officially a city, the inevitable result of rapid growth and urbanization. The city had begun to spread, and at that time the First Ward was split into two wards: First and Sixth. Soon the land area was expanded to include 3.14 square miles so that the borders extended from the Lehigh River to Seventeenth Street (east to west), and from Sumner Avenue to the Little Lehigh (north to south).

Merchants continued to find the area ripe for enterprises as diverse as boiler works and cigar factories and furniture factories. Portrait studios flourished, as did retail outfits in the Hamilton shopping district. While retail trade, crafts, and agriculture brought revenue, by the 1870s manufacturing had become the base of the city's economy. That was due largely to the prosperity of the metals industry—the Lehigh Crane Iron Company (north of Allentown), Allentown Iron Works, and others. The Allentown Rolling Mills, which originally made boiler rivets and railroad spikes, now listed the following among its products: pig metal, rolled shafting and axles, beams and angles, nuts and bolts, steam engines, locomotive turntables, and mining pumps. Iron and limestone came mostly from the county, with some iron from New Jersey and anthracite from the coal regions farther north. The Portland Cement Company, established 1872 in nearby Coplay, was another industry that spelled jobs and potential. Ultimately, the success of Allentown's industry at this time relied upon a network railway connecting the entire Middle Atlantic region.

The latest mode of transportation, streetcars, made it easy to get about town on a loop that went from Seventh to Gordon to Tenth and around to Hamilton. Some twenty-five horses gave their energy to pull eight cars and two "omnibuses."

The elegant residence of Charles Kline, Esq., stood at the corner of Sixth and Chew.

The Lehigh County Poorhouse took in twenty-four paupers when it opened in December 1845. News of the death of the oldest pauper, a feeble-minded man named simply Johnny, made the front page of the *Allentown Morning Call* on April 25, 1899. Apparently every visitor to the almshouse knew Johnny, who was "very fond of bright-colored objects and was always adorned with brass buttons."

A romantic view of Kern and Maier's Brewery.

The Allentown Fire Brick Works was owned by McHose and Ritter.

The Lehigh Tube Works was operated by Albright and Company on Front Street.

Allentown Foundry and Machine Works manufactured steam engines and railcars.

Lithographs by M. H. Traubel (Philadelphia); from a map, 1862; courtesy of Lehigh County Historical Society

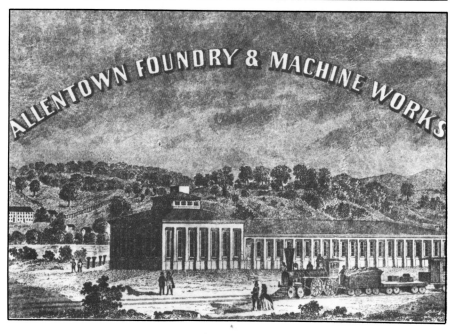

It was a time of transition for Allentown in all ways. New schools were built—boys and girls separated, of course—so that a grand total of fifty-seven schools were scattered throughout the wards in 1876, all belonging to one school district. Muhlenberg College was well under way (as of 1867), as was the Allentown Female College, which was a brave and determined response to Muhlenberg's policy of excluding women. This higher education for women as well as men was firmly established early on.

Although entertainment could be had at the courthouse, the Free Hall (now the J. I. Rodale Theater), Kline's Hall, and the Odd Fellows' Hall, Allentown's first theater came into being in 1870. The Hagenbuch Opera House, as it was known until 1885 when it closed, was on Hamilton Street above Eighth. Its existence indicates that Allentonians not only could afford to be entertained but had developed a taste for the theater.

Culturally and socially, Allentown experienced some major shifts that affected the largely Pennsylvania German populace. High German was vanishing from school lectures and church sermons, and the spoken dialect so common on the streets was undergoing a sort of corruption as English dominated the language of the business world. Furthermore, the immigration of several hundred Irish profoundly changed the nature of the community. Many of them settled in the Sixth Ward, living side by side with "Pennsy" Germans and integrating into Allentown society.

A depression in 1873 hit the banks hard and severely damaged the iron industry. The biggest companies maintained business, but it was clear that Allentown needed a shot in the arm, and resourceful business leaders looked to further diversification, the saving strategy throughout the city's history. This time the answer was silk. And what an answer it was!

The City Flour Mills were located in the Eighteenth Ward. *Stereograph, early 1870s, courtesy of* Call-Chronicle *newspapers*

The Allentown Iron Works was an extensive business which employed many people. Superintendent Samuel Lewis, who served the works from its start in 1846 until 1878, was primarily responsible for the high quality of iron produced and the general success of the company. This photograph is dated 1878. *Courtesy of Lehigh County Historical Society*

The canal connected many towns and communities along the Lehigh River, and whole families lived on barges which trucked goods from place to place. Those who lived along the river could make a business of pulling the barges with mules. *Courtesy of Pennsylvania Canal Society*

Construction workers pose along the original cellblock of the Lehigh County Prison in 1868. *Courtesy of Lehigh County Historical Society*

This view shows the completed prison, which is still in use today. *Stereograph by W. H. S. Gross, circa 1870; courtesy of* Call-Chronicle *newspapers*

Schoolgirls gathered on the steps of the Allentown Seminary at Fourth and Walnut streets in 1861. The catalog of the Seminary notes that "the boys and girls are entirely seperated (*sic*), and never meet, except at a few recitations, and at the table, at which time they are constantly under the inspection of their teachers." *Courtesy of Lehigh County Historical Society*

The Allentown Collegiate Institute and Military Academy, a private school, was chartered during the Civil War in March 1864 and continued until 1867.

In this view, students receive martial training on the front lawn. *Lithograph by Scott Eagood (sic); courtesy of Lehigh County Historical Society*

A Civil War soldier, Ignatz Gresser, reclines in camp holding hardtack on his knee. Gresser was one of the "First Defenders" and was the first casualty of the war when he was wounded in the stone-throwing at Baltimore. In 1895 he received a Congressional Medal of Honor. *Courtesy of Lehigh County Historical Society*

Civil War soldiers William and Charles Issermoyer were recorded in a tintype. *Courtesy of Lehigh County Historical Society*

Dear father,

I received your letter of the 12inst. yesterday morning soon after I had sent off my letter, so I thought I had a little leisure time I would write again, for if you are only half as glad to hear from me as I am from home I think it will be welcome. We had inspection last evening and reg. dress parade. Lieut. Col. Selfridge seems to be liked by all, he seems as a father to us. He would like to take our reg. to a camp of instruction for a short time. I think it would be needful. We are encamped at the bottom of Maryland heights, about half mile from the Potomac. The days are warm here and the nights very cold. Fire wood is very scarce, we must use fence rails to cook with, that we have done since leaving Virginia. The water is plenty for cooking and drinking. Each man has (or ought to) a tin cup, tin plate, knife and fork, haversack, canteen, blanket, some gum coats. Our

rations are shared out to each man. We get about 12 crackers (when plenty), 2 tablespoonsful of coffee and 2 of sugar, 2 of salt per day, some times beans, and a piece of pork or fresh beaf per day, about half a pound, then each man cooks as he wishes. I can do it up prime if I have it. We are often scant on a march but when we lay still a day we make up for it. We dont get much news here. I also received that paper you sent me. I would like it very much if I had a new pair of boots or shoes for I often get wet feet crossing creeks but I am afraid you cant send them just now. I suppose Lieut. Miller is still at Allentown. Capt. Huber is sick in hospital, I think at Frederick. Lieut. Hamilton (formerly orderly) is our only officer. The loss in our reg. in the battle of Wednesday, was about 30 killed & 80 wounded, so our reg. is somewhat reduced. Tell Sallie to make my small bags of thin oil cloth and roll them up like a paper and send by mail. We don't know how long we stay here, the bridge crossing the river to Harpers ferry is burnt by the rebels, so if we cross just now we must wade it. We have now slept in the open air over two weeks clear or rain and still I must say my health is much better than at home. I feel very thankful to God Almighty for giving me such a blessing. By your letter there must have been exciting times in our state and I am glad to hear that the love of country is still so great in the hearts of the Allentonians. I hope they may not have such hardships to undergo as we have, still we dont hear many complain; we only hope it may do something toward drawing this rebellion to a speedy close. I would like it if you could pass through the country the rebels have passed through. It looks very desolate especially the town of Sharpsburg, in most every house you could see holes of shot and shell. They having passed through; and along the road to here you could hardly get a piece of bread for love or money, the rebels have taken all in their hungry flight, I cant say where they are just now. Some of our boys who were slightly wounded are coming in from hospitals and are glad to be with us again. It is strange to see and hear of the narrow escapes some of our boys had in battle, some were shot in caps, haversacks, coats &c. Tell George I would write to him when I could get time but could hardly get time just now for time, paper, and stamps are scarce. Frank Keck & Charley Pfeifer are still missing, we think they are prisoners for their bodies were not found on the field. I must close with my sincere love to you all, hoping I may soon hear from you at home. The mails are not as regular now as when in regular camp but still welcome, you ought to see the beaming faces when a mail arrives and when one has a letter handed to him.

From William

—Proceedings of the Lehigh County Historical Society, vol. 22, 1958

Young William J. Reichard entered the service in August 1862 as a member of the 128th Pennsylvania Volunteers, Company G. *Courtesy of Lehigh County Historical Society*

A boy in uniform sat for this *carte de visite* ("calling card") while he was attending Allentown Collegiate Institute and Military Academy during the Civil War. *Courtesy of Lillian and Frank Gackenbach*

The first woman to hold office in the borough (and in Lehigh County) was Maria Hornbeck, who served as postmistress for eight years after her appointment in 1849. *Courtesy of Lehigh County Historical Society*

This Allentown couple struck a close, protective pose, with his hand relaxed forever on her shoulder. The oval portrait was taken around 1860. *Courtesy of Leh's Department Store*

Far more charming than any doll in costume, the child with wide eyes and shiny hair gazed directly into the ambrotypist's camera for this portrait in the late 1850s. One hand is gently poised on the table for balance. *Courtesy of Susan Weaver*

The Reverend William Helfrich was a learned Reformed pastor of the area who wrote a history of the many congregations that touched his life. He took a horse and carriage to Gettysburg to pray over the bodies of men as they lay in the fields. *Photograph by Benjamin Lochman's Photographic Gallery; courtesy of Lehigh County Historical Society*

The city's first mayor, Samuel McHose, was in office from 1867 to 1869. *Courtesy of* Call-Chronicle *newspapers*

This portrait of a young black man in a waistcoat was found in the Nathan Martin Collection and was probably taken in the late 1860s. *Photograph by Nick and Knecht; courtesy of David K. Bausch*

Local music-master Theo Foust had a music store at 35 West Hamilton Street. *Photograph by J. Jeanes, early 1870s; courtesy of Lehigh County Historical Society*

Women of the 1860s wore dresses endowed with many tucks and full skirts; hair was combed straight off the face and arranged neatly in back. *Photograph by Benjamin Lochman's Photographic Gallery, mid-1860s; courtesy of Lillian and Frank Gackenbach*

Despite snowy conditions, the Allentown Passenger Railway Company had its horse-drawn trolley out for business, traveling eastward toward Fifth Street, in this view of Hamilton Street around 1871. Left of the trolley is a horse and buggy, and at right is a Central Express wagon. *From a private collection*

A wagon drawn by horses is parked in front of M. S. Young and Company on Hamilton Street, around 1867. Young's was the local hardware mainstay for a century. *Courtesy of* Call-Chronicle *newspapers*

The American Hotel, at Sixth and Hamilton, offered a cab service from the railroad station to the hotel for its patrons' convenience. *Courtesy of Lehigh County Historical Society*

Balloon ascensions were main-street events in old Allentown. This one took place on center square in 1875. The menfolk liked to gather in small groups while women (such as the one in foreground in apron and sunbonnet) tended the children. *From a private collection*

General Frank D. Beary was a six-year-old schoolboy at the time of the 1875 balloon ascension:

I remember one Saturday the great Donaldson came to Allentown to make a balloon ascension. The great silk bag was filled with gas on center square. The balloon was covered with a network of ropes, to which was attached a large circular basket about four feet high. A group of volunteers held the ropes until the bag was fully distended and then Mr. Donaldson, dressed in bright-colored tights, stepped into the basket. The ropes were released and the balloon soared into space. It traveled southwest and we boys ran after it. Fairview Cemetery was well into the country, and by the time we reached the gateway most of us were tired—scared at being so far from home. Miss Balliett [schoolteacher] saw and recognized me. She took me by the arm, led me into her home, gave me supper, and then some member of her family brought me back to my home in Allentown.

—*"In the Beginning: Spotlights on the Early Schooldays in Allentown,"*
by J. Warren Fritsch

With horses and buggies ready to go, the Third Zion Reformed Church members congregated for the camera early in the morning before embarking on an outing—first to Dorney Park to watch the trout being fed, then off to a big picnic, in 1874. *Courtesy of Zion Reformed United Church of Christ*

The Allentown Cornet Band posed in full dress, 1872. *From the John Y. Kohl collection; courtesy of* Call-Chronicle *newspapers*

This was Allentown Police Department of 1874. At center right is Captain William H. Kleckner, chief. At center left is Mayor Tilghman Good (1874-76), who later was chief of police (1878-84). *Courtesy of Allentown Bureau of Police*

Dwell Here and Prosper
1881-1917

The Adelaide was the first silk mill in Pennsylvania, a vast structure built solidly of brick on a cement foundation. The successful venture led to the opening of several mills throughout Allentown, although in terms of size and business the Adelaide was the queen of them all. *Photograph from Allentown Illustrated, 1891; courtesy of Leh's Department Store*

The Adelaide Silk Mill announced its grand opening in 1881 with elegant commemorative silk banners, five by ten inches in size. *Courtesy of Willard Zimmerman*

*H*undreds showed up for the grand occasion, milled around, inspected, exchanged hearty hellos, and tapped their feet to the band's festive tunes. Mayors meshed with labor leaders, bankers mingled with railroad dignitaries, and the mood of the crowd was full of good humor and high optimism. All paused to take in the Allentown mayor's words:

> We now, in the name of the subscribers and the Phoenix Manufacturing Company, dedicate this building to the industry of silk manufacture, with the hope that it may prove to be the nucleus of a great and extensive enterprise in the Lehigh Valley; and we christen it in honor of the wife of the distinguished president of the company—The Adelaide Silk Mills.

The opening of "the Adelaide" on November 17, 1881, marked the beginning of a new era for Allentown. It led to the opening of several other mills in rapid succession. For many years, the silk weaving industry was to provide employment for over one-third of the city's population, so there were few families without silk-related income. Whole families worked in the mills, immigrants alongside Pennsylvania Germans from the countryside. The pay was reputed to be good, and if a person didn't like the work at one mill, he or she could walk across the street and find work the same day at another.

The initial thrust into large-scale industrialization came from the Phoenix Silk Manufacturing Company of Paterson, New Jersey, also known as Silk City.

Supported by local capital, in the name of the Silk Factory Fund, the Adelaide Mill was built in Allentown

G. Buehler and Company, in business since 1897, was the largest manufacturer of elegant furniture frames in the city, with a market in several large cities of the East. The men behind the scenes took center stage for this photograph at the brick plant at 301 North Front Street, while the boss's daughter stood graciously at the top of the steps. *Courtesy of Louis Buehler*

From the ceiling, drive shafts and belts ran the machine floor of Gottlieb Buehler's first plant. The proprietor himself stands in the center with his daughter in 1897. *Courtesy of Louis Buehler*

in the hope that it would prove as successful a venture as the Paterson plant. The original building, four stories high, 250 feet long, and 50 feet wide, easily held around 2,000 workers full-handed. The Lehigh Valley Railroad was close by for shipping and receiving.

Five years after the Adelaide was built, a second silk mill, the Pioneer, opened at North Seventh Street. The Allen Spinning Company, at Jordan and Gordon streets, also opened for the manufacture of jute yarn and twine. From the 1890s more and more silk and ribbon mills found Allentown an ideal spot to set up their looms. Eighteen ninety-three marked the opening of the Palace Ribbon Mill; 1897, the Weilbacher Silk Mill; and 1899, the Rionor Silk Mill. By the late 1920s, there were more than fifty silk mills in the city. It was an enormous business. Women in those days wore silk petticoats and dresses, and most coats had silk linings, so the demand for material was high.

Children worked in the mills, starting at about age ten or twelve. If a woman were to be widowed and left without means, it was not uncommon for her to go to work and take a child or two out of school to help supplement the family income. Working hours were long: from about 6 a.m. to 6 p.m., with a fast half-hour lunch. Allentonian Grace Frank, whose mother and two aunts (three sisters) all worked in a silk mill as winders, recalls:

> Working conditions for women were horrible. You were allowed to go to the bathroom once in the morning, and once in the afternoon. Not any time you wanted to: *once when the bell rang. . . .* And no, women were never paid what they should have been. But even men weren't paid very much. My father earned $12.50 a week at Traylor Engineering. And my parents paid $12 a month rent.

Period of Productivity

The work ethic has been expressed very simply by Allentonians: You work. From the 1880s on, the silk industry had Allentown going great guns in a dynamic period based on a marriage of technology and hard work. Several silk-related industries sprouted, such as silk-dyeing plants and bobbin works. Other industries that found their niches in the city included a plant of the Iowa Barb Wire Company, which was transferred from Easton, and Arbogast and Bastian, the first large-scale slaughterhouse here. Machines that sewed shoes together had forever changed the shoe industry as factory after factory equipped itself and began churning out shoes and boots. Cigarmaking and the cigar box industry were lucrative. And the Portland Cement Company flourished at this time, turning great beds of rock into big profit. The Allentown area was, until World War I, the world's largest cement-producing region.

There were boiler works and ironworks, including the huge Allentown Rollings Mills, which eventually became the Aldrich Pump Company in 1914. Machine

The skilled artisans of Buehler's in 1905 stand behind the fancy chair and couch sets that gave the firm a reputation for excellence. *Courtesy of Louis Buehler*

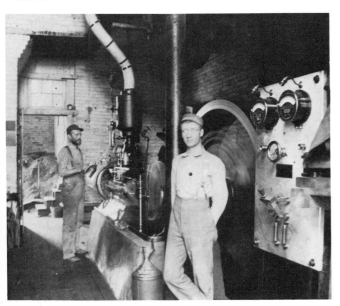

Inside the Buehler furniture factory, William Camp stands bracing the post while Alfred Geary holds an oilcan behind. The electrical generating engine pictured was Buehler's first, a 100 HP Williamsport engine, used from 1902 to 1905. *Courtesy of Louis Buehler*

shops made bronze and brass goods; planing mills handled construction needs. Furniture-making turned out good profits for several companies: Dorney's, Bear's, Yeager's, Buehler's and Schneck's, to name a few. Breweries tried to fill what seemed to be an insatiable demand, and their cousin industries of barrel and bottle works were in full swing. Horseshoe works existed side by side with auto companies, and, as yet, smithies and farriers had more work than auto mechanics.

The railroad was essential to the successful world of Allentown industrialism. The Lehigh Valley Railroad provided primary freight service to major connections, with the transport of anthracite coal as chief concern. From 1888 passenger service was tremendously improved when the Lehigh Valley Railroad built the Jordan Loop, which routed trains to a new terminal at the Hamilton Street Bridge on the Jordan Creek's west bank. Another passenger station, the Allentown Terminal Depot, was built at Race and Hamilton by the Philadelphia and Reading and the Central Railroad of New Jersey.

Industrialization had its effect on food producers then as the city's population multiplied. Farming was at its peak in the county, with almost 3,500 farm units in the mid-1880s. From that point on, there began a trend toward consolidation into larger units, and land was used for purposes other than farming. By the 1890s, farm products were definitely oriented toward the needs of the city; farmers turned away from buckwheat and flax in favor of potatoes and oats, apples, and peaches.

What with all the factories and the influx of labor, it was natural that the merchants of Allentown would step up business. Several stores, well known even today, opened their doors for business: Koch and Shankweiler (1876), Breinig and Bachman (1888), Shankweiler and Lehr (1890), Hess Brothers (1897), and Woolworth's (1889). Hess's Department Store, which now has several branch stores and continues to attract patrons from the county and beyond, was started by two brothers, Max and Charles Hess. One man who "remembers when" tells the story of the Hesses' success:

The original Hesses were, of course, peddlers through the county. They both were a little hunchbacked from carrying packs on their backs. And after they had traveled through the county, they started a store on Hamilton between Eighth and Ninth streets. The country people would come in and the Hesses would always stand in front of the store. And these country people—well, they knew them—they'd stayed at a lot of those farmhouses overnight . . . and when they'd come in, they [Hess

brothers] would greet them with "Hello, Charlie," "Hello, Amanda," and they'd see that they got a clerk to wait on them. And when they were ready to leave, they'd say, "Well, now, come back here, and you pick out a piece of cloth for a dress," and they'd give the farmer's wife enough goods to make herself a dress. Those were little things that brought people back, you see.

—From an interview with George Weiss

All in all, there was wide diversity in types of occupation. As a sampling, by 1914 there were thirty-two dry-goods dealers, sixty-five cigarmakers, eight horseshoers, eighteen ice cream dealers, eighty-three hotels and saloons, fifty-four music teachers, twenty-seven building contractors, six hardware dealers, ten photographers, 100 grocers, one taxidermist, 106 dressmakers, twelve lime dealers, four banks and four trust companies, twenty-three bread bakers (and eight pretzel makers), ten newspapers, eighty realtors, and seventy-five barbers.

Around Town

The city took on a new look in this busy time. Christmas shoppers of 1882 saw Hamilton Street storefronts lit up at night for the first time. Electricity had "arrived." A man named Roney installed an electric dynamo in his shoe factory and proceeded to incorporate as Allentown Electric Light Company (1886). Later the company was to be absorbed into the present Pennsylvania Power and Light Company (PP&L). Electric lights ablaze in Leh's store were a main attraction when the store reopened after extensive remodeling in 1891, though the steam elevators and telephones were enticing novelties as well.

Electric trolleys pushed out the old horse-and-car system early in the 1890s. They were a safe and inexpensive way to get around, and literally thousands rode the trolleys to work and about town. The first line, built by the Allentown and Bethlehem Rapid Transit Company, connected Allentown and Bethlehem. Soon other systems cropped up, finally merging into the Lehigh Valley Traction Company. By World War I, the lines extended to Easton, Phillipsburg (New Jersey), Slatington, and to Norristown, which connected to Philadelphia.

Allentown was a city in transition in the period from the turn of the century until World War I. It nearly doubled its land area by steadily annexing large tracts of land, and its main thoroughfares were paved for the first time from the early 1900s. Within City Hall the form of government itself underwent a major

The making of good spirits is serious business, or so it seems judging from these fellows. Joseph Lieberman (top left) founded the Eagle Brewery in 1864 on Sixth and Union streets. The two children are Lieberman's sons. The photograph was taken sometime in the 1880s. *Courtesy of Ray Brennen*

Tilghman Statler exhibited his fine vehicles above the porch for this photograph of his carriage and wagon works. The business, located at Sixth and Linden streets, prospered from 1842 to 1910. *From* Manual of the City of Allentown, *1904; courtesy of Marguerite Kehm Sandt*

The Grim Coal and Wood wagon is hitched up in front of the shop at 12 North Ninth Street in 1902. *From the Nathan Martin album; courtesy of Mrs. John C. Zettlemoyer*

change in 1913 as a new council of five, including the mayor, took over. Previously, government was made up of a select council of fourteen and a common council of twenty-eight. The new councilmembers were each responsible for a municipal department: Public Affairs (handled by the mayor), Accounts and Finances, Streets and Public Improvements, Parks and Public Property, and Public Safety.

The needs of the public received direct attention when several institutions got their start. Medical services in general expanded. In 1899 the Allentown Hospital opened at Seventeenth and Chew on land purchased by the Ladies' Auxiliary. In 1912 the Homeopathic State Hospital was founded on a spacious tract of land surrounded by trees and lawns; now called Allentown State Hospital, it handles psychiatric patients and operates a special division for children. Sacred Heart Hospital took its inspiration from convent sisters who nursed the sick poor. Eventually, the monsignors and sisters were able to open a community hospital in 1913 at Fourth and Chew.

The establishment of the Good Shepherd Home in 1908 meant that, at long last, there was a home for those who were rejected by society: orphans, handicapped persons, and elderly citizens. Earlier, in 1904, the Phoebe Home had been founded to care for the elderly and infirm, and both charitable homes continue in active service today.

Other notable institutions that serve the community include the Lehigh County Historical Society (1904), the Chamber of Commerce (1905), and the Allentown Free Library (1912).

The city park system, which is one of the greenest and finest of any city in America, was just beginning to blossom. While many were responsible for planning and creating the parks, there is a primary figure associated with the whole park system and beautification program:

General Harry Clay Trexler. Known as a bullish businessman (successful in lumber, cement, agriculture, and other ventures), the general was also a nature lover and generous with his substantial funds for projects he personally believed in.

The first park, completed in 1904, was West Park, which went from vacant lot to tastefully landscaped green with beautiful walkways and gardens, a fountain, and a band shell for outdoor concerts. A few years later the Department of Parks bought the land where Trout Hall stood, since Muhlenberg College was moving west, and in 1908 opened the historic Allen Park. It was just the beginning; for decades to come the city continued to develop and extend the park system.

More People, More Flavor

Allentown's population just kept right on growing along with industry. In 1890 there were over 25,000 people, and by 1920 the count leaped to 73,500. Right up until 1940 people moved in at a phenomenal rate. The mills attracted immigrants, first Germans, English, Welsh, Irish, and Scottish, and then eastern, southern, and central Europeans. In the 1910s there were firmly entrenched neighborhoods of Polish, Russian, Ukrainian, Slovak, Italian, Greek, and Syrian Allentonians.

Religious life had indeed diversified. At first the dominant Reformed and Lutheran congregations had resisted, but new denominations came in strong: Methodists, Baptists, Presbyterians, Roman Catholics, and Jews. The first synagogue was established in 1885. In 1900 a black church, the African Methodist Episcopal Church, was started by Mrs. Harriet Baker on North Penn Street.

Around town, clear divisions existed between

Like the baker and the milkman, the meat vendor delivered his wares by wagon. Customers would come out to the street, look over the meat, and point out the cuts they wanted. This early Arbogast and Bastian wagon advertised "Home Dressed Refrigerated Beef," which simply meant that there was ice in there with the meat. A & B's started in 1887 and is still a major meatpacker today. *Courtesy of Ann Scarlos*

Those who still remember say it was a monstrous fire. The Arbogast and Bastian slaughterhouse, bounded by the Lehigh River and Hamilton Street, was severely damaged on July 14, 1905. *From a private collection*

uptown and downtown. Downtown meant blue-collar and immigrant neighborhoods, where the railroad terminals, mills, and other heavy industries were concentrated. Uptown was further up Hamilton going west, where the old families and the better-off lived.

Mingo was a nickname for the Sixth Ward downtown, which was a phenomenon of its own. At the turn of the century, most of the ward's residents were Irish, German, and Jewish, and many remember it as the Ellis Island of Allentown. One well-known businessman in the ward was Jacob Max, who received his citizenship in 1893 and ran a scrap business beneath the Tilghman Street Bridge. His daughter, Esther Coleman, recalls that her father helped other immigrants get settled when they arrived by lending money for a horse and wagon and opening rooms in his house for an informal library (the uptown library was quite a distance away) and a dressmaking service. Weddings, too, became

associated with the Max family:

In another room sister Ida supervised the preparations of dinners for large weddings and meetings. This was most convenient for the newcomers. When I was very young, I often went up to the large dance hall on the third floor to watch the wedding guests dance to strange music. One strange custom [centered on] a pile of plates which were placed beside the bride. A gentleman came up to her, threw some money on a plate in order to break it. If he succeeded in breaking the plate, he had the pleasure of dancing with the bride for a few minutes. The money was then given to the bride and groom. The ladies wore beautiful embroidered aprons tied by lovely bows. I was naughty then, because I pulled the apron bows apart while they danced.

Engineer Eugene Tracy and his crew
pose aboard locomotive No. 50 of the
Central Railroad of New Jersey, circa
1900. *Courtesy of Mae Weida*

Looking down the tracks at the Allentown Steel and Wire Company in
1913. *Courtesy of Alvin Fiedler*

This detail from a panoramic view of Allentown, October 1911, looks west toward center city (right). Various industries lined the waterfront, notably Arbogast and Bastian (center left). Also visible are the gas company behind A & B, and the Adelaide Silk Mill behind the smokestack. The Hamilton Street Bridge is at far left. *From a private collection*

When the Mingo boys got together with the uptown boys for baseball or a game of ice hockey on the canal, the competition sometimes ended in a fight. No serious conflicts took place, but the resentment and battles of pride between downtowners and uptowners of any age were real. Certain businesses simply did not extend a hand to the "foreigners."

The black population of the city was small—about 100—and they too suffered from stereotyping in employment. From most accounts, blacks performed manual labor in work crews, worked for the wealthy households of the west end, or waited on tables around town. At least one man attained a position as "chef-cook" at the Hotel Allen, and another man was the only black barber in town. The bootblack (a black man) at Wetherhold and Metzgar's shoe store was remembered for speaking Pennsylvania Dutch "as well as anyone who lived in Macungie." (Macungie is a small town nearby where Dutch is still heard on the streets.) Allentonian Ruth Junius, who was growing up then, recalls that she too learned to speak the dialect in order to play with the other children. Black women did housework for rich families as well as their own families at home, and some were involved in dressmaking and other trades.

Housewifery was, in those days, a lot tougher. Cleaning outside was as important as inside. According to Grace Frank:

Every woman that lived in this end of the town [Chestnut and Second], every single morning, would get out and sweep off her sidewalk, put the dirt in the gutter, and take a dustpan and sweep it up. And once a week—twice a week if she had the time and felt like it—she would scrub her threshold and her front porch, her stoop....Yes, by some standards the women would be clean-crazy. But their houses were immaculate.

As most of the roads were still unpaved, keeping mud and dirt out was a constant struggle. William Fiedler recalls:

You wiped your shoes before you went in. Had an old scrap of rug out. Or one of those metal scrapers. And most of the time you heard from the inside out, "Wipe your clothes and shoes off!"

Keeping the house clean was one way women could help prevent their families from coming down with diseases such as pneumonia, diphtheria, typhoid fever, meningitis, rheumatic fever, and smallpox. In time of illness some went to doctors for care, and others to homeopaths, who were popular then. Homeopathic remedies were available in drugstores, and good old-fashioned home treatments were a standard. Many a

59

kitchen cabinet held Mother's favorite medicines of castor oil, sulfur, and molasses.

When a family member passed away, the home became the setting for all the events connected with the funeral, except for the burial and church services. Undertakers used ice and other materials to lay out the body. A funeral was a momentous event. Grace Frank recalls what it was like:

People made a fuss over funerals. They took pictures of the dead in their coffins: they would stand the coffin up, take pictures of the dead. People were laid out in their homes—the parlor was usually sealed off—and women would go in black six months to a year.... If it was your cousin you went six months [or] three months; if it was your father you went a year; if it was your husband, you went longer, as long as you were grieving for him.... When you had a funeral, you'd go down to say to Jimmy Bowen, "I need a ham for this day"— and he'd have it. And potato salad, of course. Pickled cabbage, of course. Then all your relatives would come to the funeral, aunts and uncles and cousins from two or three generations back. And some of them had to get up at five in the morning to get here in time for the funeral. Well, you couldn't let them go back again hungry, so you'd throw a spread. And the neighbors would donate baked beans and whatever else they had. And cake and pies till they came out of your ears. And this would not be a party exactly, but people would remember the dead because there would be a prayer offered for the peace and continuation and whatever of their soul, and then we'd sit down and we would visit. If it was in planting time [though], no farmer would leave his fields. He'd skip the funeral, and send regrets.

In warm months, only the circus or the fair could rival a sunny day spent at Central Park or Dorney Park with friends and family. The women would get up early to pack a big picnic lunch with their neighbors, and then everyone would hop a trolley to the amusement park. Central Park, owned by the Lehigh Valley Traction Company, was quite an operation with its merry-go-round, a roller coaster called the Cyclone, bowling alleys, a bingo stand, ample picnic grounds, a dance hall, an auditorium, a theater, and even a herd of buffalo in a wooded area.

Picnic outings among groups were very popular, whether it was the Bar Association or a band or a church group. At one time, the annual Sunday school outings became a topic of great tongue-wagging since the picnics were allegedly turning into "kiss-nics." Elwood Fisher, who wrote Pennsylvania German dialect columns in the Allentown Democrat under the name Solwell Files, confirmed that the picnics were indeed merry events:

May 16, 1904: We have many more Sunday schools than we had in the past, and every one wants to hold a picnic.... Picnics where the whole school congregates like one family are the best. That's where married men and women may help play "copen-hagen" and the women can learn the difference between their husbands, since one is not like another. Some chew "Polar Bear" and others "Fine Cut"; and the smell and the taste are not the same. Some slobber more in their kissing, but a dry kiss that is dusty is not enjoyed by the women.... Now a kiss isn't much when you take it, but how much trouble has it made already in families or in church! That's why some folks are opposed to it in public and sneak their kisses like some men their drinks— behind the door.

—Proceedings of the Lehigh County Historical Society, vol. 28, 1970

Going to dances was good fun, too. People traveled from as far as Mauch Chunk (Jim Thorpe) by train just to go to the dances at the Hotel Allen when dances like the waltz, the schottische, and the two-step were in vogue.

When there wasn't a dance, people had just as good a time at home putting on skits in the parlor or back yard, or just singing around a piano. Children played parcheesi or tiddlywinks and popped marbles.

The streets of the city were full of activity, even when there wasn't a parade (and there were lots of parades). There were people of all ages wheeling by on bicycles, and women pushing perambulators on sidewalks—that is, where there were sidewalks. (As one story goes, in the early 1900s when everyone was supposed to lay sidewalks and curbing in front of the house, one miserly fellow decided not to comply. Someone, however, planted corn in his dirt walk, and he was duly embarrassed when it came up.) Roller skating was in fashion among the youngsters as was hopscotch for the girls and baseball for the boys.

If the elections were on, men gathered on street corners to argue about candidates and lay some interesting bets. The day of the election results saw some strange doings on Hamilton Street. On one bet the loser had to push the winner in a wheelbarrow from Seventh Street to Ninth, right in the center of town. Another well-remembered loser had to roll a peanut up Hamilton Street with his nose.

Those were lively times in the city.

The Dannecker family's carting business was thriving after the turn of the century. Pictured with the lineup of horsepower are, left to right: Annie, Milton, Ada, Frances, Howard, and Edna Dannecker. *Courtesy of Ruth Wertman Dannecker*

Farming was at its peak in this period as more and more farmers moved toward fulfilling the needs of the urban market. *From the Nathan Martin album; courtesy of Mrs. John C. Zettlemoyer*

Charles Fritz (right) poses with an
unidentified coworker. Both were line-
men with Lehigh Telephone Company
in 1904. *Photograph by Hunsicker;
from a private collection*

A solitary figure drives his cart away from the Allentown Water Works in 1898. At one time this sedate setting bustled with life. Known as Fountain House at Crystal Springs, it was an eighty-chamber resort for summer boarders, with a large dining room, "ladies' parlors," a billiard room— even a "barber saloon." *Courtesy of* Call-Chronicle *newspapers*

The pump installed in the Allentown Water Works was built by Allentown Rolling Mills, an example of the cooperative industry that helped create a strong economy. In the foreground are Robert Rathbun, city engineer, and Joe Mason (in white), who represented the rolling mills. *Courtesy of* Call-Chronicle *newspapers*

Gus Beck, master shoemaker, sits for a restful moment in the stockroom of Farr's, a shoe factory that upheld the European tradition of craftsmanship. *Photograph by E. H. W., 1912; courtesy of Harvey Farr*

Wearing hats in the hot July sun, a work crew spreads cement to pave an Allentown street for the first time, in 1908. Jonas Ackerman's contracting firm hired mostly Italian immigrants to do the paving. *Courtesy of Rudy Ackerman*

On Paving the Streets

Columnist Solwell Files (whose real name was Elwood Fisher) often expressed the views, and fears, of the general public in his articles published by the *Allentown Democrat.* Apparently, Allentonians were afraid that paving the roads might make them too slippery to be practical:

April 23, 1900: Now they plan to asphalt Hamilton Street in the City and make the street as smooth as Put Minninger's head. That is supposed to beautify the City. Allentonians are getting as proud as a peacock, but I wonder how we'll then get up the hill [between Fourth and Fifth streets]. . . . The Traction Company offers to pay part of the cost, they say, and apparently their five-cent business is profitable. . . .

Sept. 10, 1900: Now then, the Monument Square in the City is as smooth as if it were greased with a pork-rind. They call it as*phalt*, and if you don't take care, you will fall. In winter, I suppose, when we have smooth ice that will be the place to see some performance. The street, however, looks good, by henk!

—*Proceedings of The Lehigh County Historical Society,* vol. 28, 1970

To Allentonians, the name Farr's has meant shoes and boots for over a century. White-collar and blue-collar workers pause for this picture taken inside Farr's shoe factory, where boxes of the finished wares lie stacked in the center. *Courtesy of Harvey Farr*

Sand mining was essential to the growth of the cement industry in Allentown. The photograph, circa 1910, shows the use of both early and modern means of transportation, from the wheelbarrow to the conveyor, from the horse-drawn wagon to a motorized pickup truck. *Courtesy of Mack Trucks*

Workers at Brey and Krause put aside work to gather for this portrait outside the factory at Front and Chew streets around 1912. Among other products, they made hardware for toilet hoppers, brass tubing, piping and moldings. *Courtesy of Mrs. Ed Fiedler*

George Rupp poses along with his coworkers, who stand on the cow-catcher of an electric freight car at Allentown Freight House on North Front Street near Linden circa 1914. *Courtesy of Annie Everett*

This interior view of the Hahn Motor Car Company, situated along the canal south of the Hamilton Street Bridge, was taken around 1914. *From a private collection*

Workmen of the Bradley Pulverizing Company pose amidst heavy chains and bulky equipment. Three members of the casual crew on the upper deck pulley are identified as Frank Clader, Delbert Herron, and Charles Scharadin. Below are Harvey Trout, Warren Gaugler, Charles Hertle, Frank Weaver, Mr. Horn, George Blum, and Nelson Arnold. Harry Romig was the foreman. *Photograph by Wint Studio, 1918; courtesy of Bradley Pulverizing Company*

A lone worker stands dwarfed by an immense crusher mill in the Dexter cement plant near Nazareth (now Penn-Dixie Company). Above his head runs a wide belt that turns the "Hercules" mills, and on his left is a dynamo. Cement was an important industry in the region, which depended upon local support industries such as the Bradley Pulverizing Company and the Lehigh Valley Railroad. *Photograph by White, circa 1922; courtesy of Bradley Pulverizing Company*

In July 1888 the power station at the Adelaide Silk Mill was ripped apart by an explosion. Repair crews faced the camera for this view of the damage from the southwest corner of Race and Linden. *Photograph by Victor Ogier; courtesy of Lehigh County Historical Society*

The steam ferry used to travel between the Lehigh Valley Boat Club (now the G. Henry Frick Boat Club) and Adam's Island circa 1910. Cables were strung across the river to keep the boats from being carried downstream. Today a steering wheel from one of the ferries can be seen lodged between the branches of a pin oak at the boat club. *Courtesy of Lehigh County Historical Society*

Checking in at the lobby of the Black Bear Hotel. *Courtesy of Hess's Department Store*

The Black Bear Hotel, on Hamilton Street below Ninth, was a well-known establishment run by W. R. Drumbore since 1879. (Earlier, the inn had been called the Balliet House, since 1869.) The horses that pulled the trolleys were stabled behind the Black Bear, through the alleyway where the boy is standing. *Courtesy of Ray Brennen*

Tall utility poles seemed to straggle down Hamilton Street in the 1890s. This photograph was taken looking west from Sixth Street. The Zion Reformed Church (its steeple obscured) stands on the left, the Hotel Allen on the right. *Photograph from* Allentown Illustrated, *1891; courtesy of Leh's Department Store*

Electric trolley car No. 1 of the Allentown and Bethlehem Rapid Transit Company races by the northeast corner of Seventh and Hamilton on its maiden run through the city, July 1, 1891. *Courtesy of Aral and Naomi Hollenbach*

The Allentown Band was stationed at Camp Allen, near Slatington, in 1886, when this photograph was taken. The entire band was in the National Guard at the time, as the story goes. When the guard was sent out to crush a strike in the coal regions, conductor Martin Klinger refused to take his men there. Instead, he asked that the band be discharged from the guard, whereupon his request was granted. *Photograph by Lindenmuth, 1886; from a private collection*

Men of Allentown on North Seventh Street at center square performed in a street minstrel show, circa 1890. The popularity of blackface entertainment and the influence of West Indians passing through during the years of river and canal traffic are reputed to have influenced the leisure activities of the working class in the First and Sixth wards. *Courtesy of Lehigh County Historical Society*

There were Masonic lodges, orders of the Eastern Star, the Independent Order of Odd Fellows, the Knights of Pythias, BPO Elks, the Fraternal Mystic Circle, and many others. At the turn of the century, Allentown was a center for secret societies, and when those organizations got together for a public event, they liked to do it in this city.

So it was that the Grand Castle of the Knights of the Golden Eagle of Pennsylvania came here to put on their extravaganza in April 1890. The knights set up three arches on Hamilton Street: two small ones at Fifth and at Ninth, and the remarkable thirty-six-foot-tall one pictured. The giant arch was made of muslin stretched over a frame, with pillars eight feet square at the base. Flags, shields, and Maltese crosses decorated the arch,

and at the top of the pillars were the High Priest (wearing a black uniform and holding a staff) and the Venerable Hermit, a main figure in the mysteries of the knights. Astride the horse at the arch's top was Lucifer, the Brave Sir Knight, in armor and carrying a shield.

After the welcoming speech to 350 delegates by Mayor Allison in Music Hall, the grand chief announced that Allentown resembled Jerusalem because of the Biblical names of the streams and nearby towns. The knight-pilgrims upheld Christian beliefs and were strongly opposed to anarchy and socialism.

The high point of the session was the big parade, in which twenty bands and drum corps played and over 1,500 men from various "castles" across the state marched together.

Seventh and Hamilton took on a new appearance on April 1, 1890, when the Grand Castle of the Knights of the Golden Eagle of Pennsylvania came to town for the annual convention. *From a private collection*

Christmas evergreens up for sale lie piled in the background on central square, two years before the Soldiers and Sailors Monument went up. At right is the YMCA, and at left on the corner is Dresher and Stephen Clothing Store, where Kuhns and Shankweiler later set up shop. The Second National Bank is the tall building two doors away. *Photograph by Charles F. Mosser, 1897; courtesy of Ruth Cosgrove D'Aleo*

Soldiers and Sailors Monument

Many new structures changed the cityscape in the busy years around the turn of the century, but one in particular has become a virtual symbol of Allentown: the Soldiers and Sailors Monument in center square. This tribute to Lehigh's sons who fought in the Civil War was originally to be erected on the south side of the square, but later it was decided that the monument should be in the middle of the intersection, which meant the trolley company had to pull up its tracks and re-route them around the site.

On March 9, 1899, the *Allentown Morning Call* carried the following story:

Sculptors and designers are hard at work on the bronze bas relief scenes that are to ornament the dies. Each of these will be four feet square. The one facing east will be a representation of the reunion of the north and south and will be portrayed by Federal and Confederate soldiers clasping hands under the folds of the Stars and Stripes. The scene on the west die will be after an allegorical painting of Philipotanx, the artist who painted the panorama of the battle of Gettysburg. This scene represents the soldiers of the north rising to the defense of the country in 1861. The scene is laid in Washington and represents President Lincoln welcoming the soldiers as they march through the streets of the Capital City. The First Defenders of Pennsylvania

are marching past the reviewing stand and behind them is the Sixth Massachusetts Regiment. On the reviewing stand stands General John A. Logan pointing out to President Lincoln the troops and from which state they came. For this purpose, however, the figure of General Hancock, a Pennsylvania soldier, will take the place of General Logan. This design alone cost $1200.

The scenes on the north and south sides will represent a battle between the cavalry and infantry, and the navy bombarding the artillery.

The figure of the Goddess of Liberty, flag in hand, which will surmount the shaft, will be nine feet high and will face east.

The day of the unveiling called for a grand celebration on the square: parades, speeches, and song. Allentonian John McClafferty remembers October 19, 1899:

I was a young schoolboy at the unveiling. We formed a parade and the teachers marched us up to the monument. We all had little flags. The governor made a speech and the Allentown Band played. We sang the "Star-Spangled Banner" and all, and afterwards we were marched back to school again.... They wouldn't have anything without the kids in it, you know.

Allentonians gathered in center square in 1898 for the ground-breaking ceremony of the Soldiers and Sailors Monument, which was to honor Lehigh veterans of the Civil War. *Photograph by Jeanes; courtesy of Lehigh County Historical Society*

It took a year to build the Soldiers and Sailors Monument, so vehicles and pedestrians had to take wide detours around the square. Workmen used granite from Vermont with bronze and copper ornamentation, which cost $43,000. Today, it is hard to imagine Allentown without the monument. *Courtesy of David K. Bausch*

A graceful bronze statue of the Goddess of Liberty crowns the ninety-seven-foot monument. *Courtesy of Call-Chronicle newspapers*

The militia looks in fine form for the review prior to the ceremonial removal of drapery around the Soldiers and Sailors Monument. *Courtesy of Lehigh County Historical Society*

After the monument was unveiled, the crowd pressed in to see it up close. *Courtesy of* Call-Chronicle *newspapers*

The thirteenth of October 1893 proved a fateful day for Breinig and Bachman Clothiers at Sixth and Hamilton. Fire destroyed the five-story enterprise, burning merchandise and invaluable historical materials from a museum collection which had been moved from the old Allentown Academy at Eighth and Walnut to the top floor of B & B's for storage. The clothing emporium was rebuilt the next year, leaving the former archways intact. *From a private collection*

All is spit and polish for the photographer's promise of posterity: the fire chief, his special vehicle, and handsomely groomed horse, circa 1900. *From the Nathan Martin album; courtesy of Mrs. John C. Zettlemoyer*

Fire trucks around the turn of the century were always an exciting sight, with their shining brass, the firemen in the back stoking the fire, and smoke pouring out of the stack. A fire company could be identified by the color of its horses, and the spirited beasts were long the pride of each outfit. *From the Nathan Martin album; courtesy of Mrs. John C. Zettlemoyer*

These gents in full dress were members of the Good Will Steam Fire Engine Company No. 3 of Allentown, prizewinners at a Wilkes-Barre, Pennsylvania, firemen's parade. Tall hats and bushy mustaches looked well together in October 1897. *Photograph by E. J. Jeanes; courtesy of Kathryn Walton*

Firefighters posed with their equipment in front of the old Allen Fire House on Ridge Avenue and Linden Street in 1900. *From a private collection*

The torrential rains that struck on February 28, 1902, left lower Hamilton Street and its buildings deep in water. Both railroad terminals were surrounded by shallow lakes. *Photograph by C. F. Mosser; from a private collection*

The railroad suffered extensive wreckage when the rains washed out the tracks. Some cars fell into the water, some were stuck in the banks, and at least one sailed downstream, hitting the Hamilton Street Bridge. *Courtesy of John Smicker*

When a railroad boxcar was carried downstream by the raging waters, it crashed through the understructure of the Hamilton Street Bridge. This three-part panorama is looking east, March 1, 1902. Several other bridges along the Little Lehigh and the Jordan were also destroyed in the flood. *From a private collection*

Once the waters calmed, the only thing to do was view and assess the damage—in this case, the Central Railroad bridge at Kline's Island. *Courtesy of John Smicker*

Floods

Throughout the history of the city, Allentown, though blessed with waterways, has been plagued by floods. Usually a flood begins with a long, hard rain that doesn't stop, and before long the rivers and creeks surge and churn, then overflow their banks.

Flood years in Allentown include 1786, 1839, 1841, 1862, 1869, 1901 (during which the trolley shut down and Adelaide Silk Mill employees worked long, hectic hours to save their delicate merchandise from damage), 1902, and on up to the latest disastrous flood of 1955.

The 1902 flood (pictured here) was one of the most calamitous, and it is also well documented. From the early shots of rising waters to the aftermath scenes where curious people gaze at human work undone in hours, the flood phenomenon is striking.

This flood began dramatically, with a wild rainstorm accompanied by thunder and lightning on February 28, unusual for winter. As the waters swirled ever more crazily and rose ever higher, people scrambled to get home, to secure their cellars or bail them out, to protect their businesses. By the time the flood peaked, the city was inaccessible from the south and west. Railroads were out, bridges swept away, factories closed, and the waterworks was deluged to the point that it had to be shut down.

Today the concept and technology of flood control have come to the fore, and the type of destruction that the 1902 flood caused is no longer a threat. Still, when it rains hard enough, wise drivers avoid the low spots by the river, and residents of Adam's Island keep an anxious watch on the debris floating downstream.

The whole town turned out to see President Teddy Roosevelt arrive at the Lehigh Valley Railroad Station on August 10, 1905. *Courtesy of Dr. Ralph Merkle*

Two trolleys travel west up Hamilton Street. Along with commercial signboards, the imposing structure of the Adelaide Silk Mill can be seen beyond the stone arches. *From the Nathan Martin album; courtesy of Mrs. John C. Zettlemoyer*

The Traction Company trolley was in Fullerton on its way to Allentown when this was taken on the Northampton Line in winter, late 1890s. Open platform cars were used during the summer. The trolleys were an extremely convenient way to get around throughout the valley, and it is said that conductors called out the stops in Pennsylvania Dutch. *From a private collection*

Well-dressed ladies in flowery hats lift their skirts to cross Hamilton Street in front of Ritter and Warmkessel's photographic studio, circa 1900. *From the Nathan Martin album; courtesy of Mrs. John C. Zettlemoyer*

A Walk Up Hamilton Street in the Early 1900's   *by Edna R. Hein*

The American Hotel at the northeast corner of Sixth and Hamilton Street had large glass windows and a lounge where the well-dressed men would sit and watch the ladies walk by. The ladies would all be dressed in the very best: hats, gloves and always very neat-looking. The men have all passed on. They were businessmen, lawyers, and so forth.

On the southwest corner of Sixth and Hamilton Street was Bob Good's Drugstore. He had little tables and chairs for the children. I would take my little girl there for an ice cream sundae or soda. Peters and Jacoby we called it. Petes and Jakes was also a good place for homemade ice cream and wonderful baked goods.

We also had many millinery stores, where they sold hats and handbags. Everyone dressed up in those days, and wearing a hat and gloves was a must!

The Hotel Allen was considered to be the best in Allentown.

The Globe store at the corner of Seventh and Hamilton Street was a very fine store where the clerks would place money in a little box and take it to the office, every time they would make a sale.

Allentown had some of the best eating places in the 1900s. Glick's Restaurant at Seventh and Hamilton Street was noted for their baked beans with oyster broth. That particular meal was their "Saturday Night Special."

The Superior Restaurant was a great place to meet your friends and have a light snack in the evening.

The Penn Fountain was another nice place to meet friends and enjoy their great sundaes, etc. The Stevens Brothers owned and operated the Penn Fountain. Later they moved uptown and called it the "Dolly Madison."

The Columbia Hotel at Tenth and Hamilton was also a nice place to have good food.

We had a great many movie houses. There was the Victor at Hall and Hamilton streets, the Hippodrome located between Sixth and Seventh on Hamilton, the Lyceum at Fountain and Hamilton streets, and the Pergola at Ninth and Hamilton streets. Silent movies were shown at these theaters and the music was played by either a man or woman at a piano, sitting down front. The theaters also had men who saw to it that no disturbances were made while the movie was being shown. This way everyone could enjoy the show much better.

The Rialto Theater was opened in 1920. At that time we had sound, but the pictures were still in black and white.

We had a very nice theater called the Orpheum, where they had vaudeville shows on a Saturday afternoon. If you sat on the balcony, you could see the show for a nickel!

We also had the Lyric Theater. During the Christmas holidays they had a different show every day.

We had two nice amusement parks Central and Dorney Park. Dorney Park is still in existence. Years ago, these parks had a motorman and conductor for the trolley car, which had reversible seats. The conductor would collect fares while standing on the running boards.

Wetherhold and Metzger shoe store had a sales angle; it was "The right store on the wrong side of the street." It is now on the right side!

We also had great furniture stores—Dugan and Frey, C. A. Dorney and Benesch's.

Bowen Grocery was a special treat to visit. The smell of roasting peanuts and the smell of grinding coffee was something to remember.

Kline's Store, where the girls after they made a sale, would call "Cash Girl," who in turn took the sales slip and money to the office and returned with the change.

We walked everywhere we went. Only a few had cars. They were a luxury.

We had many pawnshops.

Hamilton Street was the best place to shop. The stores were all very good. Some of the men's stores were Breinig and Bachman, Koch and Person, and Anewalt Brothers.

There was also the Owl Store, where you could charge and pay as little as twenty-five cents a week on your bill. There was a fine store called the Central Millinery.

Drugstores were many, such as Klump's, Bob Good, Martin's, and Waidelich's.

The Central Depot was down at Race and Hamilton streets. On the north side of the street there was a restaurant and the Central Hotel.

Roller skating on Eighth Street in the evening was a must. By 10 o'clock at night you were home (at least my brothers and I were). Of course, we only had one pair of skates, which we had to share between the three of us. There was no smoking or drinking. The girls and boys had parents who cared about them.

The famous Leh's lion is draped in dry goods as the sign announces "Remnants Sale Today" in the fall of 1898. The back of the photograph lists the workers' names as Tilghman Peters, Andrew Hartzel of Bethlehem, Henry Schelly of Koch Brothers, and William Grant, engineer, but did not say who it was peering out from the basement. *Courtesy of Leh's Department Store*

The interior of Leh's in 1905, looking down from the balcony. Poster boards atop bolts of fabric read "Reduced 15 Cts." and "Reduced 19 Cts." *Courtesy of Leh's Department Store*

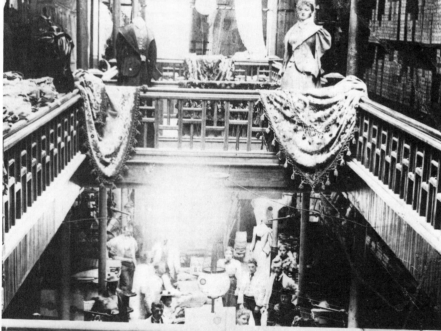

R uth Wertman Dannecker remembers that in the back of her father's oyster house there was a room like an alcove which had a coal stove:

> There Father boiled his lobsters and his crabs. He got them all alive, shipped in by train. And in the front, up to the pavement up Linden Street, the cellar went all the way out to the street. That's where he kept his barrels of oysters. He had oysters, clams, crabs, and lobsters. That's all we made. My mother could never stand fish. The smell of fish would make her sick.

The Wertmans had a very good business and later ran a restaurant. (George Wertman also had a pretzel bakery at one time.) Ruth remembers: "My mother was a very good cook. And I'm not bragging, it's true. It's like she said, if you've got a good cook, you get business."

G eorge Wertman's oyster bar at 636 Linden Street was a well-liked establishment. Out front are Mr. and Mrs. Wertman and their daughter, Ruth, around 1904. *Courtesy of Ruth Wertman Dannecker*

I nside at the counter Ruth sits like a little lady in 1906. *Photograph by Charles Ross; courtesy of Ruth Wertman Dannecker*

In a town that had sixty-five cigar-makers in 1914, Elias Kehm must have had variety enough to please any patron walking into his cigar store. Here is the proprietor himself, with his wooden Indian, outside on the sidewalk at 25 South Sixth Street.

When Elias and his ailing wife left the store to live with their son Robert, they sold everything except the cigars. Robert recalled that there were "over 3,000 twofers, five centers, and some ten-cent cigars. We took them all to our house and during the week we smoked twofers, on Sundays we smoked five centers, and on holidays we smoked ten-cent cigars." *Courtesy of Marguerite Kehm Sandt*

From one end of the bar to the other, dark brew for everyone, even the bartender. Horse races are posted one on top of the other at the left, near the fellow holding a pipe. Saloons were for men only, with their spittoons (and sometimes troughs) on the floor and "rough talk" among the patrons.

The general store carried just about everything, judging by the advertisements on the walls, from "Celluloid Starch—For Mourning Goods" and "Gold Dust—Makes Play of Housework" to "Magic Yeast—Raises the Dough." The store also provided warm relief to chilled passersby.

Photographs on these pages are from a collection of glass plates by Charles Ross who, with his wife, Linnie, photographed people in shops, schools, and factories on a documentary journey for a little over one year beginning in 1906 and originating in Allentown. Courtesy of Arthur Bransky

Inside the grocery store, in the days when the grocer cut bananas directly off the stalk.

"Not responsible for work left over 30 days," reads the sign over the counter in the back, where shoelaces hang and two pairs of shoes sit waiting for repair. A long bench for trying on new shoes is lined up in the middle of the floor, and stacks of shoeboxes sit out on the shelves.

The electrical supply store displayed globe lights, batteries, cables, generators, and countless other items for home or professional use.

Zach Boyer's butcher shop at 443 North Seventh Street was known for its bologna, scrapple and pork frankfurters. Pictured in this 1905 interior is Robert Kehm, who later opened his own shop, which he operated for thirty-two years. *Courtesy of Marguerite Kehm Sandt*

In his autobiography, Allentown butcher Robert Kehm wrote about his apprenticeship with the well-known Zach Boyer:

I must tell you how I got along with Zach Boyer. I worked for Zach for about fifteen years. He had the cleanest butcher business in Allentown, and handled the best grade of meats. He did all his own butchering and made all his own sausages and frankfurters.

When he hired me he said, "I want you to take care of my meat market, pay bills and collect my rents."

He wanted me to pay his bills because he never wrote a check. It is hard to believe that a man could do such a big business without having had any schooling. But what a memory Zach had, and at figures he could not be beat. He kept his own books and nobody else could figure out his system.

He used to get up at two o'clock every morning and the first thing he did was his bookkeeping. At four o'clock he was around the meat market waiting for me. If I was not there at exactly four o'clock, he pulled out his watch when I came and said, "Bobby, little late."

The butchers living near the shop didn't have to worry about oversleeping. If they were not at work at four o'clock, Zach was at the front door knocking and calling their names, and it was not in such a low voice either. You heard him when he came around.

*—"This Is My Life: 1879-1950"
by Robert J. Kehm, 1950*

Hess Brothers' long notions counter carried all the essentials for dressmaking. Pictured are saleswomen Gertie Miller, in front of varicolored ribbons, and Mary Mertz, near the spools of thread. *Courtesy of Hess's Department Store*

When Victor Barnes bought the Black Bear Hotel, he named it the Grand Central Hotel and in 1897 rented half of it to Max and Charles Hess for their dry goods business. *From the Nathan Martin album; courtesy of Mrs. John C. Zettlemoyer*

The pattern counter at Hess's in 1907, with salesclerk Florence Weber. Since most women made clothing for themselves and the rest of the family, we can assume this was often a bustling section of the store. *Courtesy of Hess's Department Store*

The intimate elegance of the French Room at Hess's in 1907, where fine muslin underwear was sold. *Courtesy of Hess's Department Store*

Horlacher Brewery workers at Lawrence Street, circa 1905. *Photograph
by Adam Schantz; from a private
collection*

Beneath the flags of many nations, the
Owls Lodge members dined amidst
potted palms in a celebratory dinner
on the top floor of the Hamilton Law
Building, around 1890. *From a private
collection*

Not a hunting lodge, but a center city cafe, the Metropole was loaded with a wild and woolly collection of animals, firearms, and powder horns. The back of the postcard reads, "The mounted moose was shot by myself on Saturday, October 28, 1916 at 11:45 a.m. at Wellington Lake, New Brunswick, Canada. H. O. Haas [proprietor], 837 Hamilton Street." *From a private collection*

The Anewalt Brothers Store was as well known for its big white bear as it was for its hats and furs. *Postcard published by Leo Meyer (Easton, Pa.), circa 1910; courtesy of Dolly and George Yanolko*

Outside the Metropole at Eighth and Hamilton sat a big white rabbit. *Courtesy of* Call-Chronicle

Jimmy Bowen's Grocery on Eighth and Hamilton was the type of store everyone speaks of fondly. Some remember the smell of coffee being ground or peanuts roasting; others remember the homemade cakes on Fridays and Saturdays, or baked hams and chicken. The signs on the delivery truck, which appears decked out for a parade with jack-o-lanterns and American flags, say "Our Coffees Are Cup Tested Before Bought," and "Mexican Blend—The Best Coffee for the Price." The driver is Herben G. Grim; the year, 1912. *From a private collection*

Brand-new Cadillacs, all in a row on North Seventh Street, promoted business for Dietrich Motors of Linden Street in 1914. Cranking up the Caddies to run was a trick: you had to hold the crank without wrapping your thumb around it as you normally would. That way you wouldn't get caught if the crank were to swing back suddenly. *Courtesy of Dr. Ralph Merkle*

Policeman Fred Gross operates the manual stop-go signal above his traffic booth in this 1917 street scene looking north on Sixth Street from Hamilton. *From a private collection*

HAMILTON STREET BY NIGHT, ALLENTOWN, PA.

This dramatic view of Hamilton Street by night appeared on a postcard mailed June 20, 1917. *Published by Griesemer Stationery Company; courtesy of Dolly and George Yanolko*

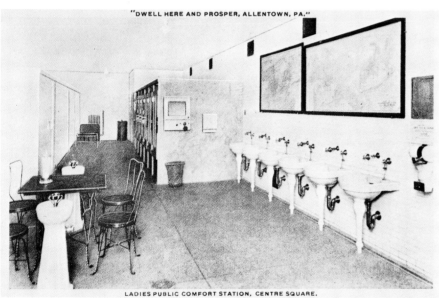

"DWELL HERE AND PROSPER, ALLENTOWN, PA."

LADIES PUBLIC COMFORT STATION, CENTRE SQUARE.

The ladies' facility underneath central square at Seventh and Hamilton was featured on this postcard of a city scene. *From a private collection*

A girl may be gay in a classy coupé;
In a taxi all may be jolly.
But the girl worthwhile
Is the girl who can smile
When you take her home in a trolley.

From an autograph album; courtesy of Annie Everett

Bankers stood under the arches of the Lehigh Valley Trust and Safe Deposit Company, adjacent to the *Daily Chronicle and News* building, around 1905. *Courtesy of* Call-Chronicle *newspapers*

Teddy Roosevelt was welcomed by 15,000 people when he spoke from the balcony of the Hotel Allen during the campaign for the Washington Party, October 26, 1914. The visit was one of several to Allentown paid by the nation's twenty-sixth president, including a campaign stopover in 1904 and a meeting at the Lyric Theater in 1912 in which he addressed the Progressive Assembly. *Courtesy of Lehigh County Historical Society*

Looking pleased with the project, officials stand balanced on the girders and ties of the Eighth Street Bridge before the concrete was poured. In November 1913 the bridge went into business, charging a penny for pedestrians to cross and between five and fifteen cents for vehicles. *Courtesy of J. William Fritsch*

The Eighth Street Bridge was built 138 feet above the Little Lehigh, stretching over a ravine to connect center city and south Allentown. Construction was under way from 1912 to 1913; when completed, the reinforced concrete structure was half a mile long and forty-six feet wide. This section is over Lawrence Street. *From a private collection*

The Theaters

The theaters of Allentown are well remembered for their fine offerings and splendid interiors. They offered vaudeville, operas, plays and dramatic skits, minstrel shows, and motion pictures. There were favorites, of course. The Lyric Theater was one of those, a playhouse that opened in 1899 at Sixth and Court streets and was known to fill every one of its 1,400 seats.

Celia Mellner, then a young wife, had the unforgettable experience of entertaining the actors and actresses in her home with an evening meal after the show. A friend of hers who had an antique jewelry store near the Lyric was well acquainted with many of the actors who returned year after year, and he liked to make deals and socialize at the same time in a private setting. So the Mellners' home became a home away from home for the traveling artists.

The actors and actresses, after the plays, would come here and have an evening meal. We were all happy, and we'd all have a cup of coffee, and I would bake and enjoy the company very much....My children grew up in that, and the family—my husband and all—would enjoy the evenings together. The actors would take their makeup off and feel at home. They would ask me what I liked best [about the show] and what I didn't, and I would tell them....

The women took interest in clothing and the men talked about something else—their rights (which they liked), politics and all that. We called each other by first names....They would come down the stairs, you know, and my stairs—they were narrow—they would dance down the stairs and act up! It was very exciting. The neighbors around here all went to bed very early, and we were very quiet so we wouldn't disturb them....Then they'd leave and go back to the hotel. Most of them stayed at the Allen Hotel at that time.

The Academy of Music, first known as the Music Hall, also offered plays and musicals with big-name talents. Allentonian George Weiss remembered how he and a buddy, George Newhard, spent Saturdays going to the Lyric and the Academy of Music, where Newhard's father was the manager. (The boys got in for free.) If they went to the Lyric in the afternoon, they'd go to the Academy at night and vice versa.

Following the afternoon show, the two Georges would go up to the Columbia Hotel at Tenth and Hamilton and get a bowl of oyster stew for ten cents, then stroll down Hamilton and stop for a quart of peanuts for a nickel. Allentown, Weiss claimed, was called Peanut Town "because you'd walk on the pavement and peanuts would crack." Then they'd take in the evening theater and afterwards check in at Mr. Newhard's office.

I wasn't allowed to come home alone and George wasn't either. We lived on Thirteenth Street at the time. So we'd meet him [Mr. Newhard] and he'd say, "Well now, boys. I ought to be busy for a half an hour or so." So we'd go up to Peters and Jacoby—that was an ice cream parlor—and get a plate of ice cream for ten cents and two ladyfingers. And that was crowded with people coming from the theater. Well then we'd spent our twenty-five cents and we'd wait for Mr. Newhard to meet us there and then we'd come home.

Well, this one particular night, we had gone to the Academy of Music that evening, and we just got home. (They'd always walk with me to see that I got to my house all right.) Walking down we heard the bell ring, and the fire company and the engine commenced to go, and golly—I went home, of course, and my folks told about this fire. Mr. Newhard said, "Well, I'm going right down" and George said, "Can we go along?" He [Mr. Newhard] in his excitement said yes, and he rushed away, and on the strength of that George and I went down....Well, that was the most spectacular fire. That thing just went up like a tinderbox. I'll always remember the horses coming and all. But that was the biggest fire I ever saw in my time.

It was 1903 when the Academy of Music burned down.

The Orpheum Theater (North Sixth Street) was another spot for popular entertainment, as were the Lyceium and the Pergola, the Hamilton and the Hippodrome. There was even a movie theater known for its Indians and cowboys, the Nickolette—otherwise known as "The Blood 'n' Thunder."

This is the splendid interior of the Lyric Theater (at left), where hundreds of musicians, actors, and lecturers appeared since its opening in 1899. Today it is the Symphony Hall. *From* Manual of the City of Allentown, *1904; courtesy of Marguerite Kehm Sandt*

"The Charming Miss Kittie Rhoades" with her "elegant wardrobe" was the opera star featured on the Music Hall bill when this photo was taken, around 1899. The once-famous theater, later called the Academy of Music, stood at the corner of Sixth and Linden where the *Call-Chronicle* building is today. *Photograph from* Allentown Illustrated, *1891; from a private collection*

The fluttering and flapping of souvenir fans must have filled the air at intermission time when the popular operetta *The Springmaid* played at the Lyric Theater in the heat of summer on August 23, 1912. Scenes from the show decorate the front; the back of the fan has space for an address (since it was also a postcard) and the following note: "This is an original production and company of 100 with an orchestra of thirty, ballet and chorus exactly as presented during its two season success at the Liberty Theater, New York, and will introduce the beautiful Hungarian prima donna Miss Gene Luneska as the saucy princess." *From a private collection*

Vaudeville was the main attraction at the Orpheum Theater at Sixth and Linden streets for its first eighteen years from 1906 to 1924. After that point, movies took over and vaudeville moved to the Colonial Theater for a while. Some of the big names that played the Orpheum included Georgie Jessel, Lila Lee, Fred Astaire, Jack Benny, W. C. Fields, Sophie Tucker, and Eddie Cantor, who described the Orpheum as a "break-in engagement" in a letter to Jack Kohl of the *Call-Chronicle*. "In other words, if you made good in Allentown, you were fine for the Philadelphias, Washingtons, Bostons and New York, etc." *From a private collection*

The Pergola was a movie theater on Hamilton and Ninth which was leveled when the Pennsylvania Power and Light building went up in 1927. Since the movies were silent, a piano player would sit up front and play scary music when the villain appeared or a romantic tune when the girl fell in love with the hero. Mrs. Buttery, at the far left of this lineup posing in 1906, was a piano player at this theater. *From a private collection*

Until 1904 Muhlenberg College held classes at Fourth and Walnut in an expanded Trout Hall. *Courtesy of J. William Fritsch*

The gymnasium at Allentown College for Women was part of some rather extensive student facilities, including recitation rooms, a chapel, library, art studio, and music room. *Photograph by W. S. Hamaker, circa 1898; from a private collection*

Men in long pants and jackets play a set of doubles on the tennis courts behind the old Muhlenberg College building. *Courtesy of J. William Fritsch*

Cooking class was part of the "thorough Christian education" offered at Allentown College for Women. As the teacher reads from the lesson, bonneted students stir and mix in front of gas ranges stretching along the table. *Photograph by Wint Studio; courtesy of Barbara Satterlee*

This is an early view of Allentown Hospital, which has remained on its original site at Seventeenth and Chew since opening in 1899. *Courtesy of David K. Bausch*

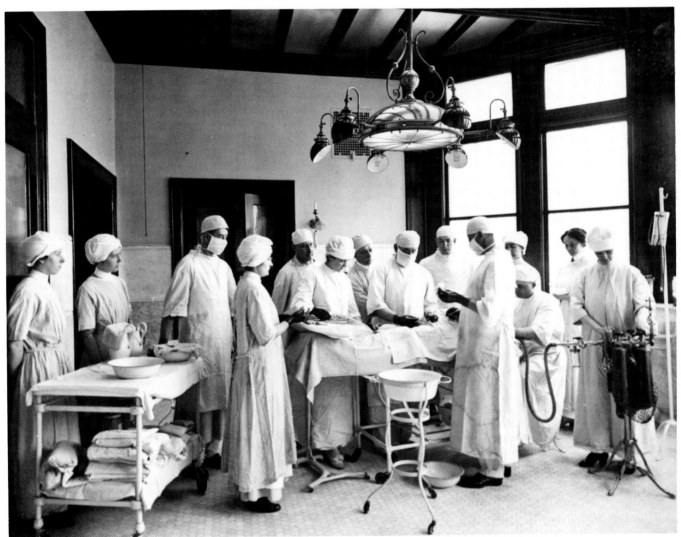

The operating room of Allentown Hospital in 1912. Short sleeves were standard, and only three persons were wearing masks. *Courtesy of Allentown Hospital*

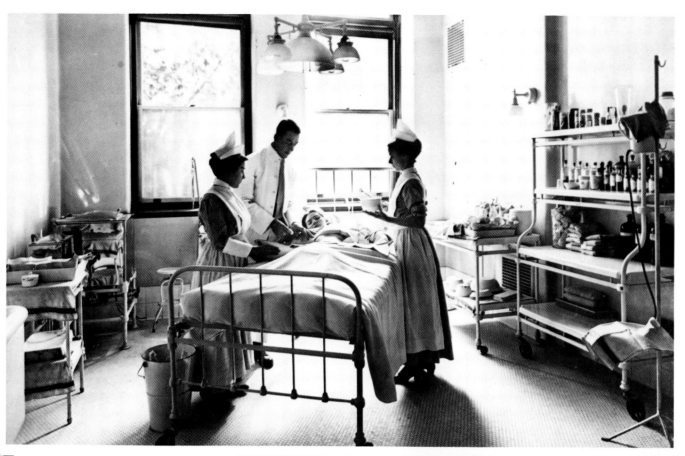

The dressing room at the hospital, around 1912. *Courtesy of Allentown Hospital*

The original Phoebe Deaconess Home for the aged and infirm was opened in 1904 at Nineteenth and Turner, on what had been the David Griesemer homestead. *Courtesy of Phoebe-Devitt Home*

The head deaconess of the Phoebe Home, Louise Whiteman (in white), was proud of her young deaconesses when they completed their nursing training in 1918 and were consecrated in the Zion Reformed Church. From left to right are: Hazel Inman, Anna Fink, Mary Weber, Ruth Bowers, Harriet Bowers, and Mabel Peters. *Photograph by Wint Studio; courtesy of Phoebe-Devitt Home*

"On the way to public school" reads the handwritten caption on the sidewalk. The Good Shepherd boys are going up St. John's Street to the Jefferson School, circa 1914. *Courtesy of Good Shepherd Home*

Five buildings of the Good Shepherd Home in 1914 are visible in this panorama of St. John's Street. Left to right: the house for crippled and blind orphans, the houses for infant orphans and for orphans and nurses (center), the laundry house (behind two trees), and the house for the elderly (far right). The home started in 1908 in a building of the parsonage at Grace Lutheran Mission. *Courtesy of Good Shepherd Home*

"God only knows my mission in this world. I am blind and am helpless and unable to move" *(Sixth Anniversary of the Good Shepherd Home)*. The Good Shepherd Home answered a long-felt need when it opened in 1908 to care for the orphaned, the handicapped, and the elderly, giving hope to those without a place in the world. A crippled orphan was the home's first charge, and soon the overwhelming need for expanded services became obvious: "The feeding of the five thousand with five barley loaves and two small fishes is not without parallel" *(Sixth Anniversary)*.

"The Blind People." *Photograph by Wint Studio, circa 1914; courtesy of Good Shepherd Home*

105

"Mother—Home—Heaven" was the message faced by those who sat in the pews of the Allentown Rescue Mission's meeting room. *Postcard, post-marked 1907; courtesy of Dolly and George Yanolko*

A solitary figure crosses the street toward the Greenleaf home at the southeast corner of Fifth and Hamilton, around 1901. *Courtesy of Lehigh County Historical Society*

Two gentlemen hitched up a sleigh to go for a drive in the snowy city streets at the turn of the century. *From the Nathan Martin album; courtesy of Mrs. John C. Zettlemoyer*

Water sprinklers kept down the dust in the days before roads were paved. The fire company provided sprinkling services to people who paid for it (about fifteen cents a week); the wagon was pulled by horses, and the driver simply lifted his foot off the sprinkler in front of houses that had not paid the fee. *From the Nathan Martin album; courtesy of Mrs. John C. Zettlemoyer*

107

Interiors at the Martin mansion at Ninth and Hamilton, in the 1890s. Needlepoint and embroidery are visible in the chair upholstery and on the pillows. In the room that appears to be Nathan Martin's study, Japanese lanterns and an umbrella mesh with fishnets and flags, and pillows are embroidered "M" and "Pipe of Peace, All Troubles Cease." *From the Nathan Martin album; courtesy of Mrs. John C. Zettlemoyer*

From the Nathan Martin album; courtesy of Mrs. John C. Zettlemoyer

From the Nathan Martin collection; courtesy of David K. Bausch

Boys ride by the fine mansions on Seventeenth near Hamilton sometime around 1912. Those who were prosperous moved west into extravagant houses, expanding the borders of the city. *From a private collection*

The Victorian mansions of west Hamilton Street were built as though the architects knew no bounds, as shown in this photograph taken around 1910. Brick, pebble, stone, even checkerboard walls, archways, balconies, veranda, windows sprouting all over—anything went. Many of the houses had coal furnaces, as indicated by the multicolumned chimneys. *Photograph by Adam L. Schantz; from a private collection*

The Rowhouses

New rowhouses stand isolated along the 2400 block of South Fourth Street, around 1914. *Courtesy of Dolly and George Yanolko*

*H*ome for many residents meant rowhouses, which are an essential characteristic of Allentown. George Weiss, who was in the slag business at the time, recalled that some of the rowhouses were built on a barter system:

Ritter and Smith were the architects and had the planing mill. Leh's owned the property. Charlie Lehr was an excavator and had horses and things and put in concrete walls. We furnished the slag for some of these houses, and the cement. A plumber did the plumbing, an electrician did the electric work. A roofer did the roofing. Well, there'd be twelve houses built. And each one [of us] would take a house, and the house would cost $5,500. Our materials—$2,000 of slag. But instead of taking money, we took a house.

Now the bank would take a mortgage on this house for you. So a man might own a house with a $2,500 mortage—or $3,000. And it was up to you to sell this house to get your money out. 'Course the laws were different. I don't know if you could do that today or not. . . . But they sold. They were well-built, lovely homes. A lot of those houses on Turner Street, right across from the West End Park, were built on that system.

*W*est Park, completed in 1914, was the city's first park. (It was also known as City Park.) Today the trees have grown tall enough to canopy the walkways with their leaves. *Postcard postmarked 1909; courtesy of Dr. Ralph Merkle*

Jennie Gackenbach looked at once elegant and demure in her ruffles and plumes. Hats such as hers were made individually at a local millinery shop. A woman would try on a hat for size and then have the milliner add different trimmings to her satisfaction. *Photograph by Ritter and Warmkessel, 1890; courtesy of Lillian and Frank Gackenbach*

Humanitarian Irene Lichtenwalner Anewalt, born in 1867, was active in the Red Cross and local hospitals. She was a charter member of the Allentown Women's Club, served as president of the Cedar Crest Alumni Association for twenty-eight years, and as a leader in the Reformed Church was sent to Sendai, Japan, in 1926 to visit colleges connected with the church. *Courtesy of Cedar Crest College*

Hat in hand, top button closed over a thick tie, big shoulders, big hands, and a resolute, manly pose suited this young man-about-town. *Photograph by Warmkessel, circa 1895; courtesy of J. William Fritsch*

A very little Mabel Mayne stood with her big Newfoundland, around 1888. *Courtesy of Liz and Ruth Taylor*

"Grandpa Stephen Lentz" was a private during the Civil War. He donned his G.A.R. hat and medal many years later to have this commemorative portrait taken in a local studio. *Courtesy of Susan Weaver*

Reverend Abraham R. Horne relaxes with his wife Jemima (Yerkes) and two grandchildren. Founder of the journal *National Educator* in 1860, Reverend Horne had a keen interest in local education, serving frequently on the school board of his ward and as principal at Muhlenberg College. This photograph was taken shortly before his death in 1903. *Courtesy of Liz and Ruth Taylor*

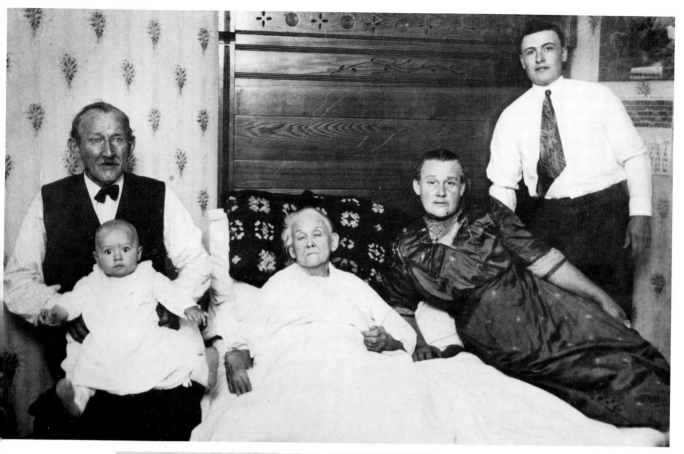

A family from "the Ward" gathers round Grandma at her bedside in May 1914, during what they must have felt were her last days. *Photograph by Adam L. Schantz; courtesy of J. William Fritsch*

Mrs. James Doherty (right) and her friend Mrs. Ellen Butz sit with good humor as their photograph is taken sometime in 1903. Mrs. Doherty was widely known throughout the Sixth Ward for her unusual generosity and genuine sensitivity to other people's needs. *Photograph by Wint Studio; courtesy of Sarah and John Schroeder*

This little fellow's outfit was as charming from the back as it was from the front. The obliging model posed in the early days of this century. *Photograph by I. R. Walp; courtesy of Lillian and Frank Gackenbach*

The winsome little girl is Marguerite Kehm (Sandt), modeling the accordian-pleated dress her mother made for her. *Photograph by R. W. Wint Studio, circa 1910; courtesy of Marguerite Kehm Sandt*

Two sides of Raymond Sherer as a lad, circa 1915. *Courtesy of Dolly and George Yanolko*

Young Sarah Rinn baked the best biscuits in the Prince Company contest, in which 300 girls competed. Her proud mother took her to a prominent photo studio in the city for this portrait. *Photograph by Lindenmuth Studio, 1913; courtesy of Sarah Rinn*

115

Every face speaks in this class portrait from the Harrison-Morton School in the First Ward. The schoolteacher is Margaret Beary, daughter of the renowned General Frank Beary. *Photograph by Adam L. Schantz, 1908; from a private collection*

Every town has its street characters, and "Schnupty" was certainly one of the most unforgettable in the 1880s. This draggle-tailed fellow (born John Ritter) was always at the wrong end of a practical joke, and he was known to shake his cane for attention if he'd passed too far down Hamilton without hearing any epithets tossed his way. *Photograph by A. Lindenmuth; courtesy of Lehigh County Historical Society*

A "Warder" in her ethnic dress was photographed around 1910. *Photograph by Adam Schantz; from a private collection*

Gentleman merchant Tilghman Statler built carriages at Sixth and Linden from 1842 to 1910. The hand-colored portrait was taken around 1898. *Photograph by Lindenmuth; courtesy of Lehigh County Historical Society*

Nathan Martin relaxes in a room that reflects his passion for Orientalism. The family mansion was on Ninth and Hamilton streets. *Self-portrait; courtesy of David K. Bausch*

Louisa Blank at Eastertime sat with tulips and hyacinths on one side and a basketful of Easter eggs on the other. *Courtesy of Marguerite Kehm Sandt*

Lizzie Kehm posed with the still wildlife of a local taxidermy shop. *Photograph by S. W. Ochs; courtesy of Marguerite Kehm Sandt*

Susan Lindenmuth quilts by her window at home, on North Sixth Street, in 1884. *Courtesy of Lehigh County Historical Society*

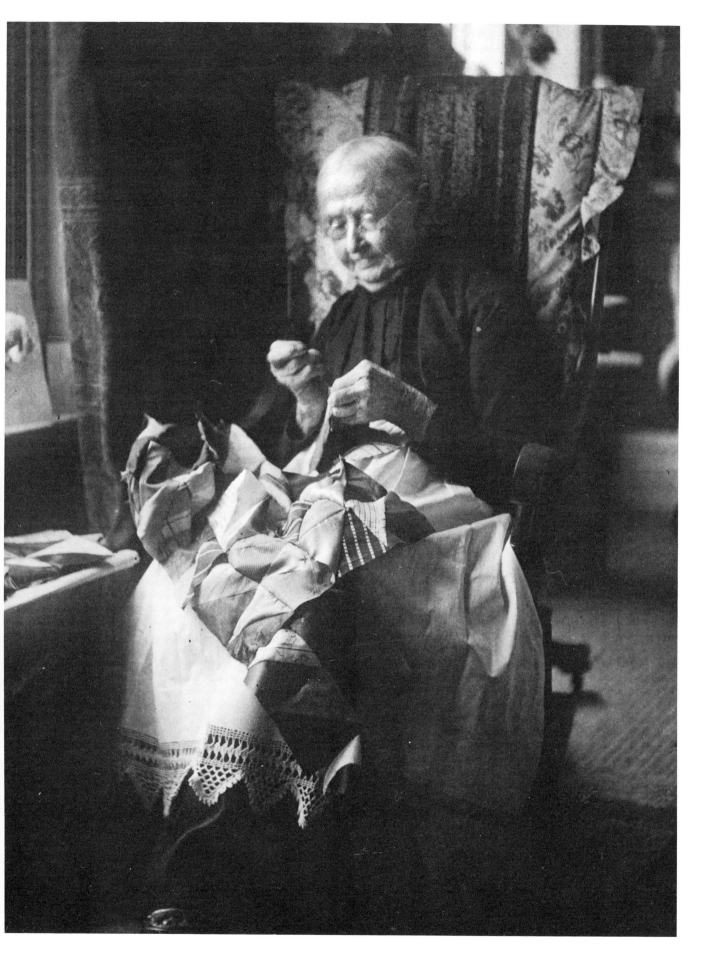

Adjutant General Frank Beary, in front of his residence on Second Street between Chestnut and Linden, cut a sharp figure astride his horse. General Beary served in the Spanish-American War and taught school in Allentown. *Photograph by Adam L. Schantz, circa 1910; from a private collection*

General Frank Beary was a schoolmaster who remembered well what it was like to be a student:

"When I entered high school in September, 1882, the whole school occupied two rooms on the third floor. Mr. F. D. Raub, later Superintendent, was the principal and Miss Amelia Grammes had charge of the girls' room. Miss Rosa Kessler taught arithmetic and algebra in the small recitation room in the front wing.

"I am afraid we caused Miss Kessler quite some trouble. One of the leaders in mischief was Harry Steltz. When something was done that drew Miss Kessler's attention she would question each boy. Harry, generally the culprit, would reply, 'I did not do nothing.' His double negative being a confession, Miss Kessler however would shake her head and remark, 'Harry, Harry, your grammar!' and then go on to question the next boy.

"During our second year in high school, we were in the room under Mr. Raub. He permitted boys to go to the hydrant for a drink, but if they became noisy he suspended the privilege. One day while I was at the hydrant some noise was made. Mr. Raub looked over his spectacles and said, 'When Frank sits down, no more boys will leave their seats.' John Richards, son of the Reverend Matthew Richards, a professor at Muhlenberg, motioned to me to remain standing. I stood at my desk and John started for the hydrant, purposely making considerable noise. Mr. Raub looked up. 'John, I thought no one was to leave his seat after Frank sat down.' He looked in my direction, grinned and said, 'Very well, since you like to stand you may do so, until I tell you to sit down.' For one week I did all my studying and reciting standing."

—From "In the Beginning: Spotlights on the Early Schooldays in Allentown" by J. Warren Fritsch

There goes Oscar! Oscar E. Kline was a familiar sight riding high on his one-of-a-kind bicycle. The American Star was heavy and difficult to ride—"You either swore at it or swore by it"—and was propelled forward by a system of levers rather than pedals. Oscar the High-Wheeler clearly mastered the technique, for he rode his Star into his eighties, long after the bike had become a true dinosaur. This photograph was taken in 1911. *Courtesy of Sara Rinn*

Ella Young had to time her shopping visits to Allentown very carefully when she drove in from Zionsville with Bert the horse. Bert was known to stand on his hind legs when the factory whistles blew at the end of the day, so Mrs. Young would have to be out of town by then. *Courtesy of Mildred Benson*

Afternoon tea with the ladies in 1903. Holding delicate cups of bone china are, left to right: Blanche Horne Grammes, "Aunt Irene" Wenrich, and Sadie Horne Mayne. *Courtesy of Liz and Ruth Taylor*

The Sweitzer sisters played chess by gaslight around 1905. *Courtesy of Ruth Cosgrove D'Aleo*

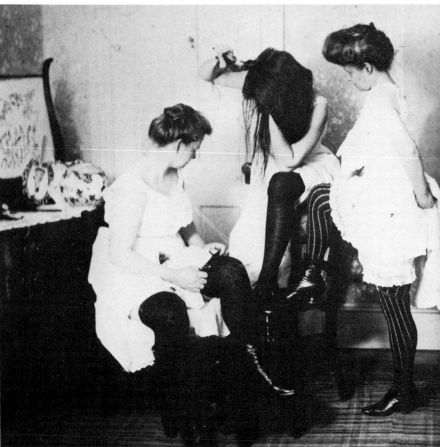

Ladies at their toilette. *From a private collection*

These young women in the 1890s were possibly classmates at Allentown College for Women. *Cabinet photograph, by Lehnart's Studio; from a private collection*

Dressed for an outing, daughter Mary wears white ruffles and carries a frilly parasol in contrast to her mother Anna Dresher Martin's dark elegance, fan in one hand and plain umbrella in the other. *From the Nathan Martin collection, circa 1900; courtesy of David K. Bausch*

The canal was not strictly a business route. Louis Tiffany, later of stained-glass fame, organized and led this photographic tour for aristocratic friends and associates. They traveled along the Delaware and Lehigh Canals from Bristol to Mauch Chunk. *From the Pennsylvania Canal Society collection; courtesy of Canal Museum*

Friends canoeing on the canal around 1905. *Courtesy of Dr. Ralph Merkle*

As the menfolk hold the bridles steady, the women pose on horseback along a dusty road around 1903. *Courtesy of Lillian and Frank Gackenbach*

This summer day must have ranked high in the good-memories category for the contented group of women and children gathered in this candid photograph taken around 1908. The identification on the back tells us only, "Front row: second lady (dark suit) from left, Annie C. Gackenbach and Lillie G." *Courtesy of Lillian and Frank Gackenbach*

A drive in the automobile was the latest in fun and fashion. It was also an adventure to sit in the open at "breakneck" speeds. This photograph of a moving vehicle and its well-hatted riders was taken around 1910. *Courtesy of Mae Weida*

Women dressed in kimonos for an entertaining skit in the backyard bring a touch of Japan to Allentown. The photograph was taken November 25, 1914. *Courtesy of Ruth Cosgrove D'Aleo*

Young and Irish, and from the Sixth
Ward. In the front row, left to right, are
Edward Reilly, James McGinley,
Patrick McFadden, and Peter Maher,
and in back, Francey Harkins and
Jimmy McHugh. *Courtesy of John
McClafferty*

Summer fun. In the cart is Ralph Esser Kline, and pulling, left to right, are Mabel Kressler (Mrs. Martin Klinger) and Mabel Stine (Mrs. Nimson Eckert), circa 1905. *Courtesy of St. John's Lutheran Church*

Thrilled by the catch. *Courtesy of St. John's Lutheran Church*

Focus is anywhere but on the food in this merry group of picnickers on South Mountain, circa 1905. At right, two fun-lovers share a banana. *Courtesy of St. John's Lutheran Church*

School chums at Big Rock, August 8, 1914. *Courtesy of Ruth Cosgrove D'Aleo*

It was a good day to paddle a canoe along the Lehigh. The photo, taken around 1910, shows Adams Island in the background. From left to right the canoers are John "Lucky" Gallagher, John Gaffney, John B. McClafferty, Frank Cannon, and Hugh Ferry. *Courtesy of John McClafferty*

Members of the One-Year Beneficial Society social club relax and pal around in a grove, drinking beer, strumming guitars, and singing. Identified is Robert J. Kehm, in the center with a long tie, next to a man in bowler hat and pipe. *Courtesy of Marguerite Kehm Sandt*

Boys at the Dorney Park swimming pool watch their pal take a dive in 1908. *From a private collection*

The people who went on this group outing (possibly to old Trappe Church) were all members of St. John's Lutheran Church and represent an extraordinary congregation of men who were well known in the community. The names are given here as remembered by Harold W. Pretz. In the back row, from left to right: 1. Arthur Keller, of E. Keller and Sons, jewelers, 2. Dr. Grim, physician, 3. Samuel Kleppinger, son of grocer George Kleppinger, 4. Joseph Shimer, associated with his father in the carpet business, 5. John Otto, 6. unidentified, 7. Frank Weil, planing mill operator, 8. Dr. Howard Seip, dentist and son of a Muhlenberg College president, 9. Edward Kron- inger, greenhouse owner, 10. unidentified, 11. Percy Fenstermacher, associated with General Harry Trexler, 12. Reverend Augustus Steimle, pastor of St. John's, 13. Charles Kech, officer with the Allentown National Bank and later treasurer of the Allentown School District, 14. Wilson Jacoby, of Peters and Jacoby ice cream parlor, 15. unidentified, 16. Werley, a tailor, 17. Schatz, grocer, 18. Milton Henninger, judge, 19. Tilghman Diehl, of Brobst and Diehl publishing, 20. John Schuon, dealer in flour, feed and coal, 21. Schlechter, relative of the printer, 22. James Holman, a teller at Second National Bank and later member of city council, 23. Charles Wagner, of Allentown Steam Heat and Power Company, 24. Edwin Keller, jeweler, 25. Reverend Steimle's son, 26. Edwin Keller, son of Arthur and grandson of Edwin, the jeweler. Front row: 27. Oscar Bernheim, treasurer of Muhlenberg College, 28. Francis Lewis, attorney, 29. Gustavus Arbogast, of Arbogast and Bastian, 30. Henry Pretz, bookkeeper at Allentown National Bank, 31. Thomas Wenner, with Allentown School District, 32. Newton Wilson, in the foundry business, 33. Charles Heckman of Allentown Trust Company. *Courtesy of St. John's Lutheran Church*

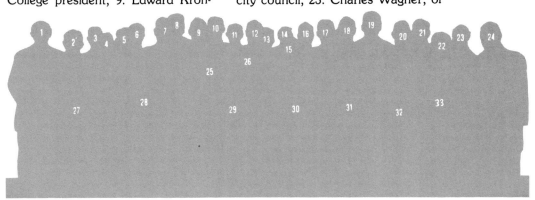

On the occasion of the first Bar Association picnic in 1917, a photograph commemorates the gathering of some of the most influential legal minds of the time. These men were lawyers, judges, congressmen, and district attorneys. Numbered from left to right, starting with the men seated, are: 1. Robert L. Stuart, 2. Fred B. Gernerd, district attorney, congressman, 3. Austin A. Glick, 4. Robert L. Schiffert. Second row: 5. Richard W. Iobst, judge, 6. chauffeur for Thomas F. Diefenderfer, 7. Earl V. Schantz, son of Milton P. Schantz, 8. Nimson Eckert, 9. Ralph H. Schatz, 10. Robert G. Kleckner, 11. Fred E. Lewis, mayor, 12. Edwin K. Kline, 13. Thomas F. Diefenderfer, 14. Samuel J. Kistler, 15. Allen Hagenbuch, 16. J. Thomas Shantz, 17. Charles W. Webb, 18. John E. Hartzell, 19. Walter Senger, 20. Lawrence H. Rupp, district attorney, 21. Dallas Dillinger, Jr., 22. John L. Cutshall, district attorney, 23. Warren K. Miller, district attorney, 24. Arthur G. DeWalt, congressman, 25. Charles W. Kaeppel, 26. W. La Monte Gillette, 27. Frank M. Trexler, judge of the Supreme Court, 28. David R. Horn. Rear rows: 29. Horace W. Schantz, district attorney, state senator, chairman pro tem of Pennsylvania Senate, 30. George W. Aubrey, 31. Malcolm W. Gross, mayor four times, 32. Claude T. Reno, judge, attorney general, superior court justice, 33. George Kuhl, 34. Morris Hoats, 35. Wilson A. West, 36. Clinton A. Groman, judge, 37. Ira T. Erdman, register of wills, 38. Francis J. Gildner, 39. John G. Diefenderfer, referee in bankruptcy, 40. Milton P. Schantz, 41. Milton C. Henninger, judge, 42. John L. Schwartz, district attorney, 43. Wilson K. Mohr, 44. James B. Deshler, 45. Charles O. Hunsicker, mayor, 46. Frank T. L. Keiter

Championship bike rider William J. Daubenspeck was one of the many local cycling enthusiasts who raced in Sunday century races—one-hundred-mile bike trips—in the 1890s. When he was not on his bicycle, Daubenspeck was working long hours in a silk mill. *From the* Evening Chronicle, *March 13, 1940; courtesy of Edith Mellner*

Fencing at the YMCA gymnasium, circa 1900. Courtesy of David K. Bausch

The North End and Bellevue baseball players were tough to tumble: they were champions of the Sixth Ward League around 1910, winning every game except for a tie in the first game. Standing, left to right, are Harmony, Hixon, Schoffer, Miller, and Eck. Seated: Heil, Miller, Drockenbroad (manager), Remmel, and Bill Harkin. Not pictured was S. S. Dornblaser. *Courtesy of Betty Harkin Brong*

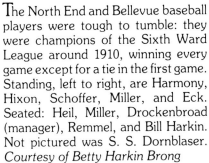

This was the Allentown High School football team of 1914. *Courtesy of J. William Fritsch*

In the Days Before Uniforms

Harry German, the so-called father of Allentown High School organized athletics, played football on the school team in 1899. He recalled:

"Each fellow had to furnish his own equipment; consequently we had a motley array of jerseys and these were not padded. The elbows took a terrific beating, and first aid was required after every contest. Helmets were just coming into use. Our fullback was fortunate to own one. Several nose guards and a few shin guards, much like the cricket guards, completed the equipment supply. Most of the players worked in street shoes without cleats. Football players in those days must have been the original 'iron' men.

"For one of the away games, the boys borrowed complete outfits from Muhlenberg College players.

It was the first time the attire of the players showed any uniformity, and the team put on a fine show. But the decision to borrow uniforms proved embarrassing for me, since a member of the opposing team ripped the jersey right off my back. Let me assure you there were no passes in 1900. We used a T-formation, with guards-back variations. The guard who was drawn out of the line carried the ball and smashed directly through the line with the entire backfield shoving like a battering ram, or criss-cross behind the center into the weaker side of the line. The backfield hit the line or dashed around ends, and the ends went around opposing ends. That was the system."

—From "In the Beginning: Spotlights on the Early Schooldays in Allentown," by J. Warren Fritsch

135

Two members of the Allentown Band, Albertus Meyers (left) and Ferdinand Soprano, pose with French horns in 1915. Meyers became the band's conductor in 1926, and in 1974 the Eighth Street Bridge was renamed after him: the Albertus L. Meyers Memorial Bridge. Both he and Soprano had played in the opening ceremony for the bridge in 1913. *Courtesy of Ferdinand Soprano*

The Jacob Max family helped organize the Judaean Band in 1914. Pictured are the brothers and cousins that made up the Max contingent of the band. *Photograph by Wint Studios; courtesy of Esther Max Coleman*

The Good Shepherd Home Boys Band with Clover, "the oldest horse in the world." The photograph commemorates the band's second tour and was taken at Catawissa, Pennsylvania. *Photograph by A. R. Johnson, 1915; courtesy of Good Shepherd Home*

The Ladies Band of Allentown came into being September 3, 1915. *Courtesy of Dolly and George Yanolko*

The Pioneer Band became a part of the Allentown band tradition in 1909. The musicians gathered in front of the Salem United Church of Christ on Chew Street near Seventh for this portrait, taken probably in 1914 or 1915. *Courtesy of Jeff Chambers*

When circuses first came to town, they set up their tents and wagons at various sites around the city including Fourth and Union streets, reportedly where this photograph was made in the last years of the site's use. From 1889 the big tops went to the new Allentown Fairgrounds in the west end. *Courtesy of John Smicker*

The Great Allentown Fair

*I*t became clear in the 1880s that the old fairgrounds site was too cramped for space, especially when it came to the races, for "speed horses" were a main attraction of the fair. Not only was the racetrack too short but more stables were needed, and the grandstand was simply too small. So in 1888 land was purchased at Seventeenth and Chew streets (the west end), and work was under way in no time. The usual exhibition buildings were built, including a huge main exhibition hall, agricultural hall and poultry hall, and ample stabling for all sorts of livestock was erected. The city water mains had to be extended west to meet the fair's needs.

Along Seventeenth Street there was a grove of trees where benches and a bandstand provided shady respite for tired fairgoers. And, of course, there was the new racetrack—a half-mile-long track considered one of the best anywhere. For the crowds, a spacious grandstand capable of seating 2,500 went up. For the horses, many new stalls.

Everything was perfect for the 1889 opening. That is, everything but the weather. All week long the rains kept people away and dashed any hopes of horse-racing. The disappointed managers did the next best thing: they scheduled a special trotting race to take place three weeks after that and prayed that the weather would hold. It did. The carefully graded track got a good trial, the horses performed beautifully, and the whole event was a big success.

Circuses, too, were held on the fairgrounds. They often came to the city in the morning, unloaded at the train station, and paraded through the streets on their way to set up the big tent.

These acrobats put on a show at the Allentown Fair around 1904. The professional show-ladies must have been quite skilled to perform stunts in such bulky costumes. *Courtesy of Dr. Ralph Merkle*

Fairgoers walk the midway past the "Pleasure Wheel" and a stand (foreground) offering "sour kraut," potatoes, and pork. *Courtesy of Dr. Ralph Merkle*

Striped awnings covered food stands, and tall painted signs lured customers into the side shows along the midway. *Courtesy of Dr. Ralph Merkle*

And then came the elephants, lumbering along between the rowhouses on Turner Street when the circus came to town in 1909. *From a private collection*

Daring and cheerful circus performers stood outside the big top at the fairgrounds around 1910. *From a private collection*

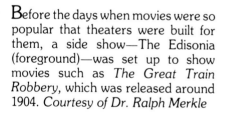

"Speed horses" with drivers race by the judges' stand at the fairgrounds as the time is posted, circa 1905. *Courtesy of* Call-Chronicle *newspapers*

Before the days when movies were so popular that theaters were built for them, a side show—The Edisonia (foreground)—was set up to show movies such as *The Great Train Robbery*, which was released around 1904. *Courtesy of Dr. Ralph Merkle*

The place is Third and Chestnut streets; the item being hoisted, an aeroplane. The event was the fearless barnstormer "Beacky" flying at the fairgrounds around 1908. *From a private collection*

These are scenes from Central Park, the largest and most popular amusement park and picnic grounds of the day. The enterprise was owned by the Lehigh Valley Traction Company, which ran trolleys that brought Allentonians straight east to the park (near Rittersville) from center city. *Detail from a panorama photograph, 1906; from a private collection*

In 1900, the carousel at Central Park relied on steam and was operated by John Ebelhauser (right) and son Philip. *Courtesy of Fred Walbert*

The Cyclone at Central Park was one of the nation's largest roller coasters circa 1915. *Photograph by C. F. Fegely; courtesy of Mae Weida*

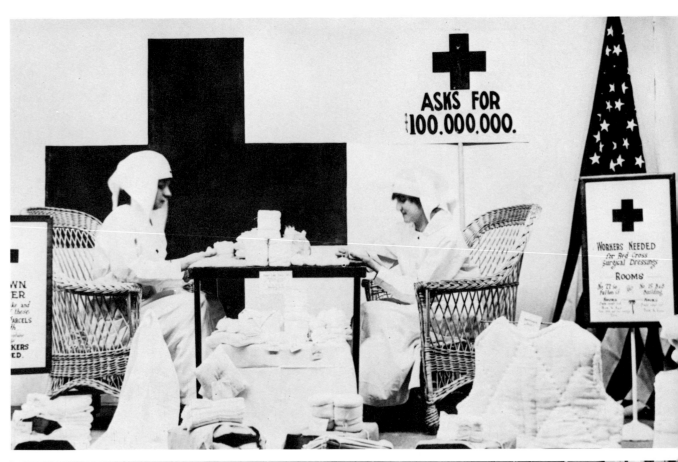

Chapter Six

The Sobering Impact of the World War I Years

1917-1918

Frances Hohl and Charlotte Nicoll, engrossed in sewing surgical dressings for the Red Cross, make a heart-warming tableau in the window of Hess's Department Store, as they appeal for volunteers. *Photograph by Wint Studio; courtesy of Hess's Department Store*

If you weren't working, they'd put you in the army. That's the way it was. You had to have some reason to keep you out of it....Men working in the Bethlehem Steel Company couldn't *get* in the army. Bethlehem Steel would have them put in Class 4 or something, so they couldn't get in the army even if they wanted it.

—From an interview with John McClafferty

So recalls one Allentonian who was working at the Aldrich Pump Company in 1917 when practically all of his friends went off to war. A lot of them didn't come back.

To the citizens of Allentown, the reality of the distant war meant that neighbors' boys were gone and their fates were uncertain; that foreign laborers were coming to the city to take up factory positions; that people's consciousness had stepped out from the country city into the world vista. Visibly, the war was Camp Crane, located on the Allentown Fairgrounds, where an ambulance and hospital corps trained in rescue and first aid techniques. And every so often a group of them would march through the streets down to the railroad station en route to overseas destinations. The children were given red roses to toss out to the soldiers.

For men and women who met on a stroll down Hamilton Street, talk centered on the war and the boys in Europe:

Everybody would talk about their sons being away, and they hadn't heard for so many months from them....And there were certain things that were going on in the war that our sons would write and the words would be cut out, just like the Second World War....We couldn't get mail so fast and there was no TV then and no radio, so we kind of had to wait. We'd wait sometimes a year till we heard from our family. For instance, my brother was here in New Jersey in a hospital, and we didn't hear from him for a whole year, if he was alive or dead.

—From an interview with Celia Mellner

The Mack "bloomer girls," so called for their work uniforms of baggy trousers, helped keep the truck factory at high production levels while the war was on. *Courtesy of Mack Trucks*

147

Obviously, communication was a drawn-out, frustrating affair. The best a family could do in these times was simply to wait.

It appears true that there were eligible men deliberately kept from the service in Allentown, men who made a contribution to the war effort through certain types of factory work on the home front. Bethlehem Steel workers seem to have qualified for a special look-aside from the draft board. Other industries that operated briskly through the war included the iron furnaces, Mack Trucks, Traylor Engineering Company, which temporarily expanded into making shells and ships, and the lumber business, cement industry, and fabric mills. Mack Trucks found fame through the war as their sturdy vehicles proved themselves all over Europe. Two brothers, John and Charles Mack, had opened the factory in 1905 after moving from Brooklyn.

While food was a little harder to get (particularly eggs and sugar) and some goods available before the war were not to be had (certain kinds of china and fabrics), most folks in the city fared well during the war years. That is, until the great flu epidemic, a nationwide calamity, struck toward the end of the war. At that time, there were no cures for pneumonia or flu, and no one knew what to do except to hang "acifidity bags" (actually asafetida), which were quite evil-smelling, around their necks. People were afraid even to go to church. One city-dweller saw evidence of personal tragedies within a working day's time:

> By walking to work, you know, you'd pass these homes. In the morning everything was okay, but by the time you came home there was a drape.... They used to have drapes on the doors at that time when somebody died.
> —From an interview with William Jacoby

Camp Crane soldiers suffered perhaps more severely than people who lived at home, for the men had no heat in their barracks.

> In the middle of the night, you'd hear the clatter of marching feet going down Turner Street as the guys were leaving Camp Crane to embark. That was the thing that hit you then [about the war years], but even that didn't hit you too much. I think the thing that hit you the most was the flu epidemic then. Gee, that was awful when that hit in 1918 and '17 at Camp Crane.... They were dying like flies out there. Most everybody [caught it]. A lot of people died from it. As a kid you'd go to these undertakers—stacks and stacks of caskets. It shocked everybody because there were so many deaths. To me, that was probably the biggest calamity at the time.
> —From an interview
> with Samuel Fenstermacher

On Armistice Day, a great din went up across the city as all the bells clanged and every whistle blew in celebration. In true Allentown tradition, there was a large parade down Hamilton Street, and the surviving soldiers returned home (although some chose to stay behind in the country where they were stationed). Unfortunately, any hopes of "the boys" sliding right into the employment scene were soon dashed. It was not that easy to get a job. The industries that continued to prosper after the war were full up with the immigrants who had moved in while native sons were away, and a number of other mills and factories shut down altogether, laying off workers by the hundreds. Many who had worked in Allentown through the war years had no choice but to leave. As for the soldiers:

> Naturally, they came back, and they thought that they were entitled to the jobs that they left because it was their hometown. They couldn't find work. So they had to leave here. They went up to the coal mines to work, and scattered around.
> —Celia Mellner

Another Allentonian concurred:

> Some fellows had a hard time getting their jobs back after the war; company wouldn't take them back. In later wars it was understood that when you came back, your job was waiting for you.
> —John McClafferty

A wire mill worker whose company turned out nails in the war and shut down afterward said that work was truly scarce. "That's why we left," said William Jacoby. "I loved Allentown. I was homesick when we moved up here." He and his wife moved to Bath where he found a job in the cement business.

The loss of family and friends in the war counted heavily in the lives of Allentonians:

> It was very sad. There were a lot of widows left.... Everything just happened so fast. And as we lost some of our families we just didn't have all that excitement, because when you lost one in the family, it really made a difference.
> —Celia Mellner

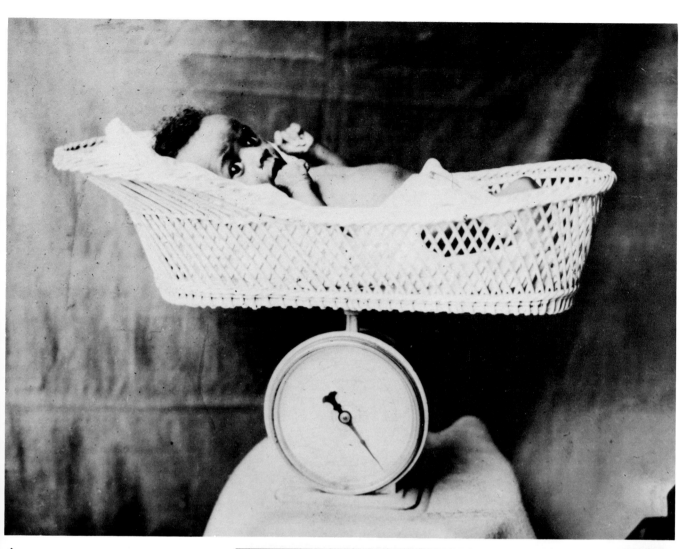

A newcomer weighs in. The Good Shepherd Home assumed care of Philip Young after both his parents fell victim to the flu epidemic in 1919. *Courtesy of Good Shepherd Home*

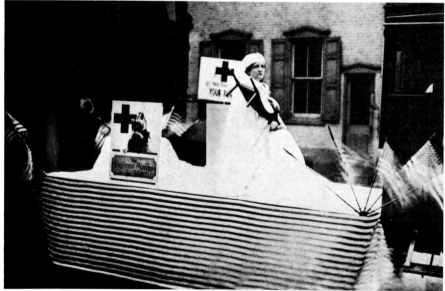

Isabel Benson glides by on a float in the Red Cross parade of May 1918, looking angelic in her role as "The Greatest Mother in the World." In real life, Isabel was the head of the mail order department at Hess's. *Courtesy of Hess's Department Store*

Thousands of well-wishers bid a fond farewell to Companies B and D, Fourth Regiment of the National Guard, as they depart for action in France on September 10, 1917. The view looks toward South Mountain from the Central Railroad of New Jersey depot. *Courtesy of* Call-Chronicle *newspapers*

Mack Bulldog trucks, under the Eighth Street Bridge as far as the eye can see, were ready for shipment to France and beyond. *From a private collection*

During World War I, the Allentown Fairgrounds was tranformed into a training base for the U.S. Ambulance Corps, and the annual fairs were suspended. Pictured is the Horse Exhibit Building, which housed training vehicles, 1918. *Courtesy of Edna R. Hein*

A troop of trainees march down the racetrack of the fairgrounds. *Courtesy of Liz and Ruth Taylor*

151

On leave, after weeks of training, these recruits are taking it easy and hamming for the camera. *Courtesy of Grace Seibert*

The soldiers at Camp Crane came from California and other parts of the country, many of them medical students and young doctors. These officers, volunteers, and mascot presented the colors for their group portrait. *Courtesy of Grace Seibert*

Children dance around the maypole at Camp Crane. Although some Romper Day activities have been dropped in favor of others, the maypole performance has become a traditional event. *Courtesy of Allentown Bureau of Recreation*

The annual citywide event known as Romper Day took place at the fairgrounds despite the war. It is very much a children's day during which youngsters represent city playgrounds in sports competitions and enjoy a day of recreation.

General Harry Trexler, standing on the platform with cane in hand along with several officials, was an originator of the program, as were Percy Ruhe and others. Behind the platform is a swimming pool where races were held, and in the foreground are boys in sports clothes. Camp Crane soldiers stand at attention in front of smiling children as parents and friends fill the grandstand. *Photograph by J. F. A. LaTour; courtesy of Allentown Bureau of Recreation*

Sailor Franklin J. Lichty was stationed on a torpedo boat destroyer. The photograph was taken December 20, 1916. *Courtesy of Hess's Department Store*

Charles Dressel posed with Old Glory before a studio backdrop of army tents. *Courtesy of Hess's Department Store*

Frederick Albright had his photo taken in 1918, while he served in the navy. *Courtesy of Hess's Department Store*

A soldier poses, cigarette in hand, for a picture taken in France and sent home around 1918. *Courtesy of Jeff Chambers*

August Soprano's portrait as a soldier in Germany is preserved in a laminated plaque illustrated with colorful patriotic images. A victim of gas warfare, Soprano died of complications in a Philadelphia hospital. *Courtesy of Ferdinand Soprano*

E PLURIBUS UNUM

Celebration decorations hung every-where for returning soldiers. This view of center square looking east was postmarked July 12, 1919. *Courtesy of Dolly and George Yanolko*

Max Hess of Hess's Department Store joins in the celebration with young Allentonians watching the Armistice Day parade, November 11, 1918. *Courtesy of Hess's Department Store*

Coming home! The reserve militia escorts a machine gun battalion coming up Hamilton Street on May 27, 1919. *Photograph by C. Wolf; courtesy of Lehigh County Historical Society*

The celebration at the end of the war
in 1918. *Courtesy of* Call-Chronicle
newspapers

Chapter Seven

Through Hectic and Precipitous Times
The Twenties and Thirties

On January 5, 1920, six former mayors gathered for the inauguration of Mayor Malcolm Gross. Standing are, left to right: Charles O. Hunsicker (1909-11), Dr. C. D. Schaeffer (1907-8), Alfred L. Reichenbach (1916-19), and Charles W. Rinn (1912-15). Seated: James L. Schadt (1899-1902), Malcolm W. Gross (1920-31, 1936-39), and Fred E. Lewis (1896-99, 1902-5, 1932-35). *Courtesy of J. William Fritsch*

Talking movies and vaudeville, World Series games over the radio, "Lucky Lindy" flying across the Atlantic Ocean—these were heady times. The years following the First World War were fast and hectic. And they were good times. At first Allentown felt the postwar recession and the depression of 1921. The demand for slate fell, and the iron furnaces were closed out by the steel industry. Various factories shut off production of wartime materials and closed down forever or turned to other products. But with growing government support for industry, things began to pick up in the mid-twenties. Jobs were plentiful. In addition to silk manufacturing, a sister trade—the garment industry—was expanding. Work on the city park system was under way and buildings were going up all over town, including the spectacular Pennsylvania Power and Light Building (1926-28), which rose 322 feet in the air. It continues to dominate the cityscape like a giant rock crystal, visible from miles away in every direction. At the time, its construction very much served to convince the last skeptics that electricity was here to stay, and in a big way.

Many people bought their first automobiles in the twenties, and, inevitably, the railroad and trolley systems began to feel the new trend digging into business. Three roads—US 309, 22, and 222—became linked to the federal highway system. In 1929 the Allentown Chamber of Commerce opened the Allentown Airport in Hanover Township. (In the 1940s the name was changed to A-B-E—Allentown-Bethlehem-Easton Airport.)

In those days, there was a certain gaiety and thrill, what with building your own crystal set and placing a 100-foot antenna on your roof. Big-band music, news, baseball, and dramatic shows entered Allentown homes over the airwaves, and the first local station (now WSAN) began programming in 1923 as WCBA.

William Fiedler was one of many entranced with radio:

I sat many a night till 3, 4 o'clock in the morning to see how many stations we'd get in...KDKA out of Pittsburgh, WOR....I'd sit there with a pencil and mark down what station I got and what time. And what was on the program. Oh boy.

It was always exciting to go to the traveling medicine shows and see the snakes. And when the circus came to town (including such big-name outfits as Barnum and Bailey), it was a day off for everybody.

Dancing was more popular than ever, and the dance floor was revolutionized when new "wild" dances like the Charleston came along. Ruth Junius is pretty sure that Allentown saw the Charleston for the first time when she "brought it back" from the school she was attending in New Jersey:

I was a Charleston queen. I really could do the Charleston. I learned it away at school, and so I came home as a bigshot, you know. So I was teaching my friends here to do the Charleston. And then later on, after I came out of school, they had a program here in Allentown, and each nationality was supposed to represent what they did, and we represented Christmas night in the South, and I did the Charleston. The *Morning Call* critic said that I made a very good [actress]. I was supposed to be an aged person but, they said, when I danced that's where I spoiled it became I was too limber. That was the *Morning Call* criticism. But they thought it was very good. Actually, I had an aunt in her seventies, and she was very good at it herself.

This was also a grand time for sports, when baseball, basketball, and football teams formed among neighborhood gangs. A & B slaughterhouse provided pig bladders for footballs, and the Hogans, the Belmonts, Triple A's, the West Ends, and the Hackers were names of just a few local teams.

Allentonian John McClafferty wrote that those were the days when:

The local barber dropped the subscription to the *Police Gazette* since women started getting their hair bobbed.

You could kiss your girl without getting lipstick all over your face.

You could take your girl to a movie and dinner and still have enough change from a $5.00 bill to buy her a box of candy.

Men wore two-piece bathing suits. If a fellow showed up with nothing but swim trunks he was ordered off the beach.

Half the people in town still kept chickens in their backyards.

Prohibition ruled the land, and everybody was barred from the cellar when the dad was making the hooch.

The horses were still the arch enemy of the street cleaners.

During church services if anyone dropped more than a quarter in the collection basket, all eyes lifted to see who was the stranger in town.

The Twenties - Time of Opportunity

There were opportunities to be had in the twenties. Success stories that could not have happened much earlier became possible then. The events that went on in Ferdinand "Fred" Soprano's life in Allentown depict just such a story. Italian-born Soprano had lived in Allentown since 1905, when he and his father and brother had come here to find jobs on the advice of an Italian friend. At first, fourteen-year-old Soprano worked at a silk mill. During the First World War, he got a job at Bethlehem Steel on the promise that he would play in the company band. He was already in the Allentown Band. At another time he looked for work at a shoe factory but was rejected when the owner discovered he was Italian.

In the early twenties, Ferdinand Soprano went back to silk, and in 1922 he got his big break: he began fixing looms at the mill. The other loom fixer there was a Pennsylvania German named Wilson Dankel who soon was a fast friend, and before long the two considered going into business for themselves.

In those days there was such a big demand for silk goods. There were big opportunities. So one day Dankel said to me, "Let's go in business for ourselves. I know that we could get work right away." And I said, "I haven't got any money to go in business. How much will it take?" "Well," he said, "we ought to have at least $12,000 to start." Mind you, none of us had any money those days. "Well, neither do I, but let's start to save now." I was getting $40 a week those days and so was he. So we started to save money, and in one year I saved $1,000. So did he. Well, now, we can't go into business with $2,000; it takes $12,000. So I said to him, "I have my house paid for. I can go to the bank and can borrow to get a mortgage," a $4,000

mortgage, which I did. So that's $5,000. Now Dankel had a friend, a brother of his wife, who was a sick man and living all by himself. So he took care of him. And he said, "Wilson, when I die, I have this railroad insurance, and I'll see that you get that money." So that's what happened. He died. And Dankel got $4,000 from this insurance. Then we both had $10,000—$5,000 each.

Now, we couldn't go into business with $10,000, so Dankel said, "Fred, would you mind if I asked my brother to be a partner in this business?" I knew his brother. He worked as a loom-fixer, too. So we asked him, and he said, "Oh, yes. I'll gladly go along with you. But I don't have any money. I can't match your money. But I have a friend who has money...." This friend of his loaned him $5,000. So we went in business.

There was a small mill in South Allentown. Somebody else went in business there, but instead of buying new looms, which we did (we knew that we could turn out first-class goods), he bought old looms, and he couldn't make it go. So he was sheriffed. It was two partners, one Irishman and one Italian. They decided to burn down the mill. They did! They soaked the floor with waste soaked in oil, and they started a fire in this mill. Luckily it didn't work, and they were both put to jail.... So this building was idle for a long time, and we knew the owner of this building. We went to him and he said, "Oh yes, you can gladly have it." And we paid then in monthly installments until we paid it off. So we started in this mill.

The DSD Silk Company opened in 1925 and stayed in business until 1957.

Little Mae Fegely tunes in the new radio. *Photograph by C. F. Fegely; courtesy of Mae Weida*

An art deco window display of the late 1920s. *Courtesy of Hess's Department Store*

The date: March 21, 1928. The occasion: the first transatlantic telephone call at Hess's Department Store. Standing, left to right, are Claude Whitner, George Sell, and John Diefenderfer. Making the call is A. L. Reinhard, with Solomon Hoffman sitting next to him. *Courtesy of Hess's Department Store*

Workers from the park department tend the foliage on the streetlight standards near the Lehigh Valley Railroad Station in the 1920s. The view looks west along Hamilton Street. Flowers and greens still adorn center city streets today. *Photograph by Detterline and Boyer; courtesy of Allentown Bureau of Parks*

"First of All, You Eat"

Unfortunately for the citizens of Allentown and the nation as a whole, the free-wheeling economic situation, in which the common man speculated and then speculated more, was to turn sour when the stock market crashed in 1929. For Allentonians, the thirties were years of uncertainty. While they did not jump out of windows, the people were deeply sobered by the shock. For quite a few, personal fortunes deteriorated or were entirely eliminated. Half the banks in the city closed their doors. The dollar bill wasn't worth anything any more, so people used paper tokens, or "script." There were strikes over pay, and "scab" laborers were sometimes harassed in the streets, mainly in the First and Sixth wards. Houses couldn't be painted or kept up as before, and some people found it impossible to pay the rent, which led to animosity between tenants and landlords. But as one resident put it, "I've always had the theory that, when you get money in, first of all, you eat."

When the Depression hit, William Fiedler was working in a silk mill:

We all asked for a quarter cent a yard more for material, for what we were getting per yard. It was piece rate. And of course we didn't get it so we went out on strike. . . . I worked in nearly every silk mill in Allentown, just to keep a job . . . because I was only earning about thirteen dollars a week.

The general weavers' strike in the late spring of 1931 almost put mill owner Ferdinand Soprano out of business. Strikers from the coal district came down and picketed, refusing to allow any workers or Soprano himself into the mill. The window panes were smashed by stones. In the end, the workers went back to the mill for less money, tired of no work and no income.

Allentown school teacher William Genszler recalled:

As teachers we took a cut in pay during the Depression. One year I didn't get paid until October—from spring. The school district didn't have the money. So in July when the tax bills went out, they started giving us something, and it took until October till we caught up with our pays.

Fewer jobs, lower pay, and having to "make do" with less were realities of the Depression years. But Allentown seems to have gotten through without suffering major trauma. (One indication lies in the absence of "Depression" photographs taken here, whereas photographers seeking evidence of hardship found plenty to document in Bethlehem and other nearby areas.) Without a doubt, the First and Sixth wards were hard hit, as were the poor in the riverfront sections. But there was fuel and food to be had. Community and family support were strong. And

163

Allentown's diversified industry proved a big bonus in the crunch. Among the main employers were the silk mills, Mack Trucks, Arbogast and Bastian, Trojan Powder Company, Lehigh Structural Steel, Traylor Engineering, Pennsylvania Power and Light (a regional operation), and others. Also, the government's Works Progress Administration (WPA) projects put many to work and kept families fed.

John Smicker recalled that there was no problem getting fuel for the winters, as there were two railroads that carried coal to the city. Coal left its mark on him as a boy:

> Three-hundred sixty-five days a year, in the thirties, when the coal mines were going full blast, the water was [full of] *black* silt. And every time you went in for a swim, and you come up and you thought you were clean, when you went home and went to bed, your mother fixed the bed in the morning and found the coal silt in there. That's when you got another licking.... That was real dirty. The bottom of the river bed had at least two feet of coal silt for many years.

Allentown never found itself in desperate straits for food since the city was surrounded by farms. Many residents grew gardens in their backyards and in vacant lots. William Genszler recounted his experience:

> When we moved here, there was a vacant lot next to us. Everybody had a vacant lot, and we had beans, carrots, onions, corn, tomatoes.... Everybody tended their own. About three families had plots on the lot across the street, and there were about three of us at another one. Of course, we dug it by hand with a spade, raked it, cultivated it by hand—we didn't have cultivators—did everything by hand. We carried water over there in a bucket to water the plants. We ate what we had, and if we had more than what we could eat, we canned it.

On the street where Edith Mellner lived, sharing food became commonplace, although somewhat a delicate matter:

> Everybody helped everybody out. If we had food, and we knew that our neighbors didn't, there was always a way of giving it without making them feel that they got something free. It was always, "Some of the farmers came down to my father and they gave him something," which sometimes did happen. "They gave him a lot of vegetables. Would you like to share them?" Refrigeration wasn't what it is today, and you knew it would spoil.

More than a few city-dwellers tell tales of feeding men who came to the back door looking for a handout,

a practice continued from the twenties. Those who gave what they could often had their fencepost or doorway marked in some way by the men who received a meal, a cue to other hungry hobos.

Some Allentonians recall that they ate "a lot of fried potatoes," and that for fifteen cents a person could get a big meal at the rescue mission or Community Hall. At the schools, a full lunch cost fifteen cents, and if the student couldn't afford that, he or she could eat for free. The city had its share of soup kitchens, too. Allentonians Liz and Ruth Taylor remember peeling potatoes every day after school for the soup lines at St. John's Lutheran Church, which was as famous for its penny movies as it was for its daily fare of potato soup, bread, and an apple.

The movies didn't cost even a penny if you didn't have it. Instead of money, you could write a prayer on a piece of paper, with a drawing, if you liked, and present it for admission.

People remained ever resourceful in making their own brand of sunshine in the midst of this economic eclipse:

> My mother would gather all the kids from the neighborhood in during the summer, and we'd sit out in the dining room and she'd read *Tom Sawyer* or *Huckleberry Finn*. She'd march us all over to Big Rock or down to Jordan Park. All the kids in the neighborhood went in and out of this house. [During] high school days—after basketball, football games—we'd come home, Mother would roll up the rugs, and we'd dance. She played the piano. And we had a victrola.
>
> —From an interview with Liz and Ruth Taylor

If you didn't dance at home, you could always hop a trolley out to a dance at the Hotel Traylor, Mealey's Auditorium, Central Park, or Dorney Park, where the big-band sound drew big crowds. Where you went depended on where your "set" went: "The Ward" had its own favorite spots downtown, and most blacks headed for Bethlehem on a dancing night. Social clubs continued as they had, though with tighter budgets, and through the will and efforts of family and friends, people got by.

Things began to look up with Roosevelt's Works Progress Administration and the National Recovery Act. The park system, especially, received a tremendous boost from the WPA. For two years men labored to develop the three parkways, Little Lehigh, Cedar, and Jordan, and completed work on Fountain Park and Riverfront Park (now Boyle Park), projects that would otherwise have taken fifty years to accomplish. The Trexler Foundation, established in 1935 after General Trexler's death, further augmented the WPA park projects, since 25 percent of the foundation's yearly earnings were to be channeled into park development.

Trexler funds could then be used in conjunction with WPA, so that land around the East Side and South Mountain reservoirs became parks, and a mosquito-infested swamp became the twenty-two-acre Union Terrace Park, where people could fish, picnic, and enjoy stage performances. The recreational facilities called Irving Park and Roosevelt Park were also WPA projects.

The Chamber of Commerce (established in 1905) put on a drive to attract new industries and succeeded in creating some 1,600 new jobs. Garment industries, including knitting and hosiery mills, were the most responsive, for they were aware that Allentown already had a work force skilled in the needle trades. At the same time, some of the silk mills began to pull out and move South. Silk as a whole was hurt by the economy and by labor troubles, as well as by other fibers that began to take over. As one longtime silk mill worker put it, "Coal died to oil; silk died to knitting. Competition's the story." Though briefly revived during the forties, the silk industry soon learned that its great days were over.

From 1920 to 1940, the city's population reflected the swing of the period. From a population of 79,000 in 1920, the figures swelled to nearly 100,000 in 1928 and then dropped to 96,600 in 1933, at which point the numbers remained fairly stable. And times continued to be tight right until the country entered the Second World War.

This Mack fire truck from the twenties belonged to Allentown Fire Department No. 12. At the wheel is Howard Dannecker. *Courtesy of Ruth Wertman Dannecker*

On January 23, 1926, fire broke out at the well-known Lafayette Hotel. The conflagration brought tragedy to many: thirteen people died, and thirty-two guests were injured. After the fire, weary firemen had to be hammered out of their coats, as ice had frozen shut the metal claps. *Photograph by Call-Chronicle newspapers; courtesy of Allentown Bureau of Inspections*

The Central Vulcanizing and Tire Company at Tenth and Turner, also known as Smith and Peifly, was one of the earliest auto supply stores when it began in 1911. There are tall gas pumps at right; at left the staff stands in front of stacks of tires. *Photograph by Wint Studio, circa 1928; courtesy of Smith and Peifly, Incorporated*

Cedar Beach was the perfect place to be on a leisurely day in July 1924. After a swim, one could change at the bathhouse (background) and take a stroll or sit under a shady tree. *From a private collection*

This late-summer view of Cedar Beach along Cedar Creek looks opposite from Muhlenberg College in 1925. The houses beyond show early westward expansion of the city, and as yet Hamilton Boulevard did not extend this far. *From a private collection*

Cooling off in Jordan Creek, mid-July 1924. *From a private collection*

A repairman at Smith and Peifly tunes up an automobile in the 1930s. *Courtesy of* Call-Chronicle *newspapers*

The Flapdoodle Band played for Central Park's big dress-up Mardi Gras, held each year on Labor Day. *Photograph by C. F. Fegely, circa 1920; courtesy of Mae Weida*

Mr. Burkhard, Central Park's manager, dressed up as an Indian chief. *Photograph by C. F. Fegely, circa 1925; courtesy of Mae Weida*

Lucille Rohrbach, a local lady, modeled one of the elaborate creations of "the world's fastest dressmaker" during a week-long entertainment held at Central Park. *Photograph by C. F. Fegely; courtesy of Mae Weida*

It was standing room only at the park's open-stage auditorium.

Picnicking in the grove with the rumble of the roller coaster close by.

A bridge arches gracefully over a slow-moving stream, a quiet spot amidst the busy scene at Dorney Park.

The slopes at Dorney Park were lined with cars in the 1920s. Folks could always take a trolley, though, if they did not own an automobile.

Photographs of Dorney Park courtesy of Robert F. Ott

Precocious formalities were belied by youthful faces and a flower in an ear in the 1920s. *Courtesy of Lillian and Frank Gackenbach*

Pennsy-Dutch flappers—Bertha Kehm, Althea Sherer, and Bessie Hoffmann—posed at Dorney Park's Castle Gardens around 1924. *Courtesy of Dolly and George Yanolko*

Syrian-American cousins Harvey Raad and Mike Saby were looking sharp. *Courtesy of Rose Joseph Moser*

With Love to Elizabeth

Let's tell it now:
Don't wait for the sunshine tomorrow, or the
moonlight tonight from above.
Young hearts were not made for sorrow;
Let's not delay any longer—
Everyone must know of our love.
Should we wait till the last gun has sounded
and the seas have cast up their dead?
Should we wait till our dear ones have all passed away,
and our lives are all worn to a thread?
Don't wait for the golden harvest
or the robin's return in the spring.
Don't wait for the day when we're all old and gray,
So let's tell of our love today.

*Written by John McClafferty for his
wife on their wedding day, April 25,
1923*

The wedding party looked unmistakably twenties—and very happy. From left to right: groom John McClafferty, bride Elizabeth Dougherty, maid of honor Frances Dougherty, and best man John McFadden, on April 25, 1923. *Courtesy of John McClafferty*

A portrait of the Joseph family in 1923 shows (left to right) children Abe, Rose, and George; mother Elizabeth; and baby Sam. Father Kamel stands next to an uncle who was visiting from Syria. *Courtesy of Rose Joseph Moser*

171

Bundled up against the cold, baby Ruth Cosgrove D'Aleo smiles from her carriage on an outing along Linden Street on March 14, 1920. *Courtesy of Ruth Cosgrove D'Aleo*

Pennsylvania German George Ruoss was the kind of relative two little boys could look up to: he had been through the Civil War, witnessed the Industrial Revolution, lived through the influenza epidemic of 1918, and seen World War I come to an end. By the time this photograph was taken in the 1920s, nothing must have surprised him. *Courtesy of Ruth Wertman Dannecker*

Stylish clothes and a thirties pose—Ruth Abraham on the Union Boulevard Bridge in 1936. *Courtesy of Rose Joseph Moser*

"Another City of 100,000 Population Added to U.S." is painted on this automobile, which carried Uncle Sam on horseback. All of Allentown celebrated in the Jubilee Parade of 1928, when the population nearly reached the six-digit mark. By 1930, however, the number had dropped to 98,000. *Photograph by M. L. Frantz; courtesy of* Call-Chronicle *newspapers*

A U.S. Navy dirigible cruised over festive Hamilton Street. *Courtesy of* Call-Chronicle *newspapers*

Turnen and Liederkranz was a German-Austrian social club that held periodic fun-filled exhibitions of acrobatics and music. The balancing act here took place in the early 1920s. *Photograph by Wint Studio; courtesy of Mrs. Ed Fiedler*

Girl Scout Troop No. 1 was organized January 29, 1920, at St. Andrew's Reformed Church, and in August the girls all went to camp at Shee La Foo Cottage on Saylor's Lake in the Poconos, where this group shot was taken. *Courtesy of Marguerite Kehm Sandt*

The Jewish Community Center basketball team in 1922 was composed of, back row, left to right: Jacob Rosenberg, Max Coleman, Sam Becker, and Jacob Max. Front: David Levy, George Feldman, N. Sontag, and "Brooks" Mandell. *Courtesy of Jewish Community Center*

Members and officers of the Oakmont Tennis Club, circa 1930, posed in their whites. Back row, left to right: Herb Hilton, Everett Palmer, Orbs Trexler, and Harry Wieland. Front row: Robert K. Schantz, Jim Fuller, Mark Harnish, and Dr. John D. Shankweiler. *Courtesy of Mrs. Florence Wieland*

This view shows the grounds and clay
courts of the Oakmont Tennis Club at
Twenty-first and Allen streets in 1924.
Courtesy of Mrs. Florence Wieland

A drugstore, the Pergola Theater, and a piano company once stood on the corner of Ninth and Hamilton before the PP & L building went up. Freeman Jewelers was spared, however, and remains a well-known place of business. *From a private collection*

General Harry C. Trexler—military man, businessman, and philanthropist—was a powerful figure who lived from 1854 to 1933. He had his hand in just about every big-business pie: he was in lumber, cement (Lehigh Portland Cement Company), and agriculture. He effected the merger of the telephone companies into Bell Telephone and the merging of trolley companies into the Lehigh Valley Transit Company, and he helped create the Pennsylvania Power and Light Company with headquarters in Allentown. *Courtesy of* Call-Chronicle *newspapers*

Steel work was in progress, May 2, 1927. *Courtesy of Pennsylvania Power and Light Company*

The completed Tower Building is the only structure in Allentown that really "scrapes the sky." *Courtesy of Pennsylvania Power and Light Company*

Tower of Power

Allentown became the regional headquarters for the Pennsylvania Power and Light Company in the mid-1920s through the efforts of General Harry Trexler and others who recognized the potential of the business, which was only ten years old then. As office space around town was already cramped, it was obvious that the company needed a central location. But few Allentonians would have believed the enormity of the venture about to be undertaken: the building of a skyscraper that would rise 322 feet, or twenty-three stories high, right in center city on Ninth and Hamilton.

A New York firm was called in to handle the job, and work began in 1926. With Allentown's base of porous limestone and abundance of underground streams, workers had to dig deep and then fill in with tons of concrete. By the time the Tower Building was completed on June 30, 1928, materials added up to a total of 3,300 tons of structural steel, 2.8 million bricks, forty-two miles of piping, and 1,400 windows and doors. Company employees found themselves with a superb view, lots of space, and a very pleasant lighting situation—natural light streamed in through the many windows to augment incandescent globes. And, just for the record, the elevators (at the time) were the fastest-moving elevators in the country.

Stonemasons Alfred Miller and John Kline.

Morning Call Model Home

I n 1930 the *Morning Call* newspaper set out to build the kind of home that any American would be happy to live in—with the latest in modern conveniences and pleasing decor. Rooms included a master bedroom, a second bedroom, a library, bathroom, kitchen, dining room, sunroom, living room, stairwell, and garage. Each function of constructing the building was performed by a different subcontractor, who was photographed and advertised. The site chosen was in the far west end of town at Twenty-eighth and Chew streets, reflecting an early trend toward moving away from center city—a trend that accelerated in the late forties and fifties.

F our rooms of the *Morning Call* Model Home portray living ideals of the thirties. The model kitchen (upper left) was done in green tile and featured a breakfast nook. Conveniences included an electric range, dishwasher,

and refrigerator.

The dining room (upper right) had a colonial flavor, with enamel wall panels that framed velour flock paper. The library (lower left) was finished entirely in walnut. The master bathroom (lower

right) on the second floor had lavender tile above an autumnal base; the shower had a glass door, and at the other end was a sunken tub.

Photographs courtesy of Call-Chronicle *newspapers*

City engineer Carl Sharle leads his staff in this portrait of March 1931. With the worst of the Depression yet to come, city workers had to plan projects with limited resources and reduced manpower. *Courtesy of Rudy Ackerman*

Workers assembled at the Allentown Fairgrounds in the morning to receive assignments and divide into crews. Timekeepers stood at the entrance to the buses that drove the men to WPA worksites. *Courtesy of Robert H. A. Laudenslager*

Laborers, some with lunches in hand, take a break on their WPA worksite. *Courtesy of Robert H. A. Laudenslager*

Constructing walls as part of the development of the Rose Garden in Cedar Parkway was among the many projects sponsored by the Works Progress Administration. *Photograph by* Call-Chronicle *newspapers; courtesy of Allentown Bureau of Parks*

Thirty-four years after her unveiling, the original Goddess of Liberty from the Soldiers and Sailors Monument came down from her pedestal for a trip to the repair shop. Here, she dwarfs a real lady standing beneath. In 1959, the elegant Miss Liberty was removed again and auctioned off as scrap. Five years later the present Miss Liberty took her place. *Photograph courtesy of* Call-Chronicle *Newspapers*

The trolley cars of the Lehigh Valley Transit Company and Liberty Bell Limited serving Philadelphia were housed beneath the skylights of the Fairview Carbarn, later used by LANTA (Lehigh and Northampton Transit Authority). This interior was taken in February 1939. *Courtesy of Railroads to Yesterday*

These Lawrence Street rowhouses in the shadow of the Eighth Street Bridge were already condemned and slated for demolition in 1938. Their backyards show that life went on despite poverty. *Courtesy of* Call-Chronicle *newspapers*

Wheelbarrow races were held at Harrison-Morton School in 1938. *Courtesy of Allentown Bureau of Recreation*

Standing in front of the Colonial Theater on Hamilton Street is the popular Schnitzelbunk Band, circa 1935. *Courtesy of Rudy Ackerman*

Champions for the 1936 season, Freeman's Dairy basketball team and a friend commemorate their achievement. *Courtesy of Allentown Bureau of Recreation*

Betty Harkin poses with her dad (behind counter) in Bill Harkin's popular beer and sandwich bar in the thirties. *Courtesy of Betty Harkin Brong*

Freeman's Dairy still delivered milk by horse-drawn truck in some areas of the city throughout the thirties. *Courtesy of Ruth Cosgrove D'Aleo*

The 500 Club enjoyed a good game of cards and sunbathing in 1938. From left to right: Althea Sherer, Mary Kemmerer, Rachel Schreiter, Marie Greenawald, Dorothy Cope, Florence Scheirer, and Etta Schneck. *Courtesy of Dolly and George Yanolko*

Electra was performed at Cedar Crest College, Spring, 1934. *Photograph by John A. Kubil; courtesy of* Call-Chronicle *newspapers*

With the assistance of professional circus people and school personnel, children designed and performed their own circus as part of WPA recreational activities. *Courtesy of Mrs. Ed Fiedler*

Recreation projects of the WPA included basic nursing classes, cooking classes, crafts classes, playground activities, as well as English language courses and citizen acculturation programs for recent immigrants. *Courtesy of Lehigh County Historical Society*

There was a mix of ages, talents, and ambitions in the early days of Walter Emerson Baum's art classes at the Lincoln School around 1942. Today the Baum School has become a recognized institution of art education. *Courtesy of Baum School of Art*

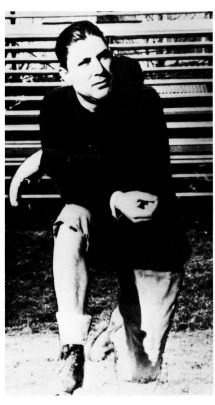

J. Birney Crum, culture hero of sports afficionados throughout the Lehigh Valley, guided Allentown High School's basketball and football teams to a total of 680 wins during his twenty-five year coaching career, from 1925 to 1950. *Courtesy of J. William Fritsch*

Officers of the Three Oaks Riding Club on Oren Boyle's land at Cedar Crest Boulevard in 1940 were, left to right: Robert Good, Lloyd Harlacher on Freddie, John Monahan, Dr. Ralph Merkle on Dolly Dimples, and Earl Wentz. *Courtesy of Dr. Ralph Merkle*

POULTRY

Four generations show off their prize
poultry at the 1930 fair.

This man exhibited his rabbit at the
1930 fair.

There was more to the fair than plump chickens and the amusement stands. This jungle character was a side-show feature in the 1930s.

Happy prizewinners in the agricultural division of the 1932 Allentown Fair.

Photographs courtesy of Call-Chronicle *newspapers*

191

Chapter Eight

The World War II Effort and Industrial Revival

When the United States entered the Second World War, the conflict that Allentonians had been following in the newspapers and over the radio was suddenly theirs. Many young men went off to fight. Industries turned again to making wartime goods. Bethlehem Steel boomed (many of its workers were Allentown residents), as did other industries such as Mack Trucks, Lehigh Structural Steel, Trojan Powder, and the garment mills. Consolidated-Vultee Aircraft built torpedo bombers, using 3,500 employees. At the Pioneer Silk Mill, the manufacture of khaki uniforms for the army took priority over the gossamer threads. Women, who had long been employed in city factories, stepped into still more openings in the work force, and men took some jobs traditionally "reserved" for women. There were male sewing machine operators, for instance. As Allentown industry swung into full gear, the area quickly became essential to the war effort.

Thousands of miles away in Saipan, a young soldier from Allentown felt a warm wave from the home front the time his landing craft infantry had to set up pontoons in order to cross a river. His flesh prickled with goose bumps "as big as peas" when on the uncamouflaged equipment he read "LSS Co."—Lehigh Structural Steel Company. "It was hairy," recalled John Smicker, one of the lucky ones who survived not only Saipan but the fierce struggle of Iwo Jima. "I was thrilled. It felt like my own backyard at home."

Allentown factory workers had, during World War II, an advantage that most laborers during World War I did not have. For the first time, great numbers of workers in large-scale industries organized into unions. At Bethlehem Steel, the United Steel Workers gained a foothold (1939); at Mack Trucks, the United Automobile Workers union came in (1940); and the cement employees joined forces with the United Cement workers. Other industries rode the tide of organized labor, and the economic and political life of the city was permanently delivered from the old status quo.

On leave during World War II, a soldier pals around with his hometown buddies. *Courtesy of Dolly and George Vanolko*

Given the German ties of the population within the city and in the surrounding region, it seems that, while most citizens were devotedly patriotic and pro-Allies, there was nonetheless an element of pro-German sympathy which occasionally manifested itself in the form of minor sabotage within industry. Machine parts would come through the assembly line painted with swastikas, for example.

Before the country entered the war, in fact, there was a Nazi camp not too far away (in a rural area of Sellersville), where reporter Gordon Fister and a photographer from the *Morning Call* went to hear a speech by Fritz Kuhn, the leader of the German-American Bund. (The Bund was a pro-Nazi organization of the thirties.) Braving Nazi "storm troopers" who tried to evict them from the grounds, the two men finagled their way into the rally where hundreds sang Nazi songs and waited for the main address.

When the famous speaker told those assembled—in German, of course—that "Adolf Hitler would lick the whole world," the crowd cheered. That is, all but the newsmen covering the story. They got out as quickly as they could to tell what they had heard, only to struggle with news bureaus who felt that their story was too unbelievable or, more probably, too controversial to print. Yet only a few years later, once the nation was at war, Allentown papers were carrying notices that any "enemy aliens" who had failed to register would face internment.

For the residents of Allentown, the war period seems to have been a tense but quiet time. While there was plenty of work, and therefore more money to be had, there was also gas rationing, so people stayed close to home, went to the parks, and listened to the radio to keep up with the war news.

Not only were the usual eggs and sugar harder to get, but meat was scarce as well. Dorney Park's Robert Ott told of how the amusement park suddenly had a run on one of its standard concessions:

> There were a lot of meat shortages. But we had a good "in" with A & B, the meat packer in town, because we'd been doing business with them so many years. We would have hot dogs when nobody else would have them, so people would come out here and just buy the raw hot dogs, pay the full price. 'Course at that time a hot dog was, I guess, five or ten cents. They'd take the raw hot dogs home and have them for dinner.

Another item that was rationed was photographic film. One photographer, who was in the processing and supplies business in the downtown area during the war, recalled that film was very hard to obtain. One time he desperately needed film to photograph the casket of a little girl who was killed in a bus accident. (It was once common to photograph funerals.) There wasn't a strip of film to be had through any of the usual channels. Finally he located a source; he bought the film from a local dentist. Most of his assignments, however, were of a lighter nature, including family portraits for sons or brothers and a fair amount of photos of Allentown ladies posing in the nude for their husbands overseas. All part of the war effort.

The end of the war brought celebrations all over town. The scene in the Sixth Ward, recalls Rose Moser, was one of exuberance:

> When the war ended, there was one big party in all the town. Cars couldn't even move in the streets. The streets *jammed*. People came out of corners all over. People were *wild*! It was like the wildest New Year's party you ever saw. *Every* Tom, Dick and Harry covered the streets. Tilghman Street was covered with people. It went on for hours....People went wild, just screaming and hollering, "The war's over! The war's over!"

The mood of the city had turned. Life came back. The dark days of the Depression and the fierce fighting of the World War were behind. Soldiers returned with stipends of about twenty dollars a week for a year, so as to get settled again.

Prior to World War II, when Europe was rearming, Allentown's Frank Buchman, a minister, proclaimed that what the world needed was a moral and spiritual rearmament. War, he said, solved nothing; peace and understanding will come about only if people follow an absolute moral standard as revealed by inner conscience. Buchman's ideas took hold as a worldwide movement called Moral Re-Armament, whose followers still make "pilgrimages" to the Buchman house on Eleventh Street. *Courtesy of* Call-Chronicle *newspapers*

Home and Health

Throughout the 1940s, life's two most basic events, birth and death, were physically transferred from a familiar setting to the outside. Women were now having their babies in the hospital instead of at home with a doctor or midwife. And funerals were moved to the neutral ground of the funeral home.

Also in this decade, significant advances made in the area of public health were beginning to take hold, meaning less disease and suffering for Allentown residents. Inoculations were being used to fight such diseases as diphtheria and tetanus. In times of flooding, mass typhoid injections were given, and quarantine placards were placed on doors where there were cases of diphtheria and other sanitation-related diseases.

Sanitation was indeed a problem, and Dr. Joseph Bierman and other public health officials made efforts to troubleshoot in sewage facilities, restaurants, and private homes. This preventive approach was met with resistance, and progress was slow. Rheumatic fever was another problem, treatable only by aspirin until the early fifties, when penicillin came into common use. From that time, medical advances continued at a fast pace, affecting the health of all Americans.

Ambitious Years

Postwar industry underwent marked changes. Certain industries involved in war products, such as steel, continued to find a market throughout the Korean conflict. Cigars and silk, though, met their demise. The railroads started dropping their coal service as oil and gasoline took over, and both the railroads and the trolleys lost passenger traffic to automobiles and buses. In June of 1953 the Lehigh Valley Transit Company ran its last trolley car, and the tracks were pulled up around town.

The arrival of Western Electric in 1946 brought a new kind of industry and a new impetus to the industrial and business life of Allentown. Skilled laborers, people with advanced degrees and engineering talents, were in more demand than ever. With Western Electric came Bell Laboratories, which also required trained personnel.

Air Products, a Detroit company making industrial gases, relocated operations to the outskirts of Allentown after the war, in order to be closer to the industrial markets of the Northeast. The company's founder was Leonard Pool, whose brainchild of the "on-site" concept of producing and selling gases developed into a multinational corporation with over 16,000 employees.

Allen Products Company, better known as ALPO, made its first big step in the dog food business during the postwar period as it moved from a garage to a manufacturing plant and began selling outside the state.

In the nearby town of Emmaus, J. I. Rodale's dreams about natural, healthful living had jelled into two magazines, *Organic Gardening and Farming* and *Prevention,* in the period from 1942 to 1950. The publications became the cornerstone of Rodale Press, which has had a major influence on the Allentown professional community.

A cultural milestone in the community's history was marked in 1959 when the Allentown Art Museum moved from its original building near the Rose Garden to its large, permanent location at Fifth and Court streets. The museum had been incorporated in 1939 with the receipt of the John Kress collection.

In the fifties Allentown modernized and urbanized. Old Home Week, celebrated in 1950, ushered in the 100,000 mark in population. Money was more plentiful, and the "movement west" began. Forsaking center city, those who could afford to do so made an exodus to the suburbs to spread out, settling on private lots with lawns and garages, mostly west of Seventeenth Street and south toward Lehigh Parkway.

The Boys from Company B

The World War II saga of the 213th National Guard Regiment is reminiscent of the First Defenders' experience during the Civil War. The men of the 213th were called up to defend the United States in February 1940, long before we officially entered the war. Frank DeChristopher (front and third from the right) recalled what happened to his outfit:

I don't know quite how it happened. We just came back from New York, on maneuvers. Boy! what a good gang. You know, anybody in our outfit could have been an officer, 'cause we were like cadets. We were really trained men. We were coming back from New York, and we thought we were going home. You know, we never got home. We got back to Allentown, yes, but I only got to see my parents for a couple minutes to say "So long!" and kept on going.

From here we went for one-year training. We thought we were going to be gone for one year. Meantime, Hitler's going like hell over there. We were mustered then. We're no more National Guard. We're *Army*. The government took over.

Full-service time.

From here we went to Virginia Beach—Camp Pendleton. Then after we left Pendleton we went to Georgia—Camp Stewart. . . . We were in Georgia during Pearl Harbor. We were down there, in Georgia, almost a year. [One day] we packed up all the tents and everything, packed it together, put it on the trucks, got the guns together, and we went to New York. And where do you think we went? Far Rockaway. Rockaway Beach!

They had a gun setup. The Germans were coming in, in there—we saw GUNS in New York! They [the Germans] were in the waters already; the subs were out in the water. Now, if you would check the history, the German subs were all over the area. They were going like a son of a gun, the Germans. But let me tell you something: They were some outfit. The Germans were good soldiers, good fighters. . . .

Now we're up there, our guns are set up, and we're protecting New York City. The whole outfit. The whole regiment. Guard duty. . . live ammunition. This is war now.

A romantic stroll on the bridge of the "Boulevard of Broken Dreams"—alias Union Boulevard—for Rose George and sailor friend "Scrubby" home on leave from navy service. *Courtesy of Rose Joseph Moser*

Thumbs up and geared up, the boys of Company B, 213th Regiment of the National Guard, ham for the camera before leaving the valley in August 1940. *Courtesy of* Call-Chronicle *newspapers*

From New York, the 213th went to Camp Kilmer, Fort Dix, and Miller's Field in New Jersey, and to Staten Island. In November of 1942 they went straight to North Africa, to Casablanca, where their ship was caught in a major sea battle off the coast for ten days before the men could land. The 213th was now part of the Second Army Corps, manning antiaircraft guns.

From Casablanca they went into the desert: Hitler's troops had been there since 1935. DeChristopher recalled the time the Second Corps was stuck "in front of the front":

The English were behind the Germans, chasing them [toward us]. They forgot we're in here. Now you talk about being in front of the front....We were told to fix bayonets. Bayonets! We used bayonets in training, but I never killed a guy, and we didn't want to either....We get our guns down to zero—point blank....It was quiet; we heard nothing. Orders came down the line to march. We had to dig up now, get the guns out of here, and go. In a half hour, we're rolling. All our outfit. Head for the hills, camouflage, and hide. You could see the Panzer division going by. We stayed quiet. *Then* we got behind. We saved lives.

In Africa the Second Corps took 40,000 prisoners.

Then they went to Salerno, Italy, a battle DeChristopher remembers as "the picture of hell." When they arrived at dawn on September 9, 1943, there were "ships as far as the eye could see." The ocean was burning from the gasoline of planes shot down in dogfights. The corps lugged their heavy artillery ashore and got stuck on the beach. The fighting went on for days. "But we held our positions and moved up," said DeChristopher. On to Naples, Rome, and Corsica.

We had to clean the bodies off the roads. Germans, Italians, Americans. There were two waves before us. I knew the Germans were the enemy, but we're all human [in the end].

Then Marseilles, where they all became MPs. In France the group began to split up. DeChristopher went on to Frankfurt, Munich, and Bonn, where he did MP duty and helped in the cleanup. On his arrival home by bus, in Allentown's Sixth Ward, he was greeted by all the neighbors. And his father brought out wine for the whole busload of fifty men—"on the house."

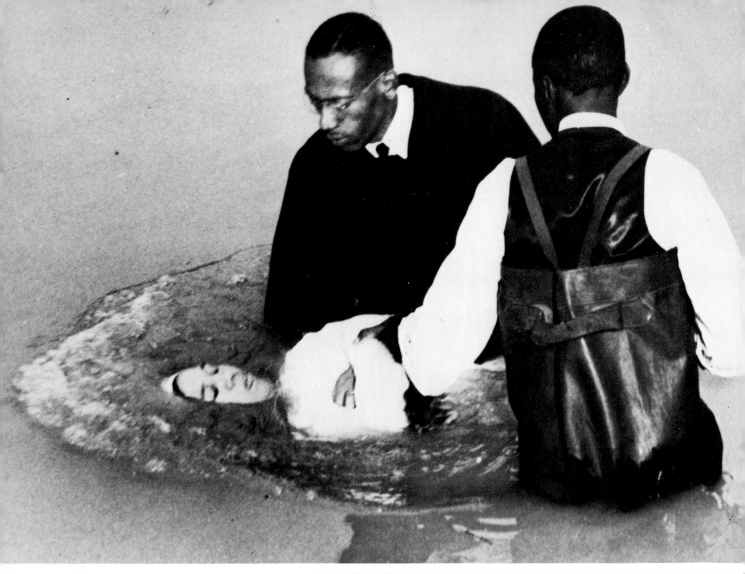

Biblical name and religious tradition come together as Reverend Horace A. Melton, with the assistance of the church's first deacon, baptized Viola Frisby in the Jordan Creek. *Photograph courtesy of Reverend Horace A. Melton*

The early congregation of the Union Baptist Church proceeds to its first baptismal rites on June 8, 1947. *Courtesy of Reverend Horace A. Melton*

Looking for the Unchurched

Reverend Horace A. Melton had the kind of initiative it took to build a church where there was none, the kind of pioneering spirit that characterizes the beginnings of many Allentown institutions. The founder and pastor of the city's black Baptist church, who came from Philadelphia to start a mission here, tells how the parish got started:

> I don't give myself any credit, nor the people. I'm very grateful to the people and I'm very thankful to the Lord. We move out in faith; God does the work. I came here knowing no one. I knocked on doors. There was one existing black church, St. James A.M.E. Zion Church on Fourth and Union streets. I said to the people, I am not here to solicit membership from persons who already have membership in the existing church in the community. I'm here looking for the unchurched, the uncommitted. And eventually there were seven persons who came together and got started: held meetings with regularity and had prayer meetings and Sunday worship services.

The first service was held in 1947 at 377 Union Street, and the first baptismal service for thirty-two members took place in the waters of the Jordan that summer. When urban renewal wiped out the Union Street location, the church moved to 621 Linden Street, and later to Sixth and Chew, where it is today.

The Union Baptist Church was established with just seven people after the young and determined preacher Horace Melton went door to door to build a congregation in 1947. *Courtesy of Reverend Horace A. Melton*

Days of redevelopment cost the city some historic buildings and familiar sights—in the name of progress. Here is the northeast corner of Fifth and Hamilton, where the Lehigh County Courthouse, City Hall, and the Allentown Art Museum now stand. In the alleys behind the ill-fated Acme, demolition has already begun. *Courtesy of Betty Harkin Brong*

Air Products came to the area in 1946. In the late fifties, Air Products built its sprawling facilities in the midst of farmlands just outside Allentown. The Trexlertown campus was composed of an administration building (foreground) and manufacturing plant (center left). Though located in the suburbs, Air Products brought many people and new growth to the city. *Courtesy of Air Products and Chemicals*

The evening headlines read, "Reagan Wins City," when television and movie star Ronald Reagan visited Allentown's General Electric small appliance plant in 1957 as a promotion for the company. Donald Gleason of employee relations shakes hands with Reagan as plant manager Clifford Flower looks on. *Courtesy of* Call-Chronicle *newspapers*

Workers assemble electron tubes in the early days of Western Electric, late 1940s. *Courtesy of* Call-Chronicle *newspapers*

The common stock of Air Products and Chemicals in Trexlertown was listed on the New York Stock Exchange on November 13, 1961. Then-president of the exchange G. Keith Funston (center) greets Leonard B. Pool (left), founder of Air Products, and George F. Pool, vice-chairman of the company. *Courtesy of Air Products and Chemicals*

In the Christmas hustle-bustle of 1951, rainy, slick streets reflected headlights, Whelan Drugstore, and the upper stories of the PP&L building. *Courtesy of Railroads to Yesterday*

Charles and Joyce MacKenzie watch their newly purchased television set with their sons, Charles and Bruce, in 1947. *Courtesy of Marge Grabias*

Don Miller of the *Call-Chronicle* initiated the Park and Shop system. "Three hundred steps from car to counter" was the local merchants' slogan. In the car are Harvey Farr of Farr Shoes, mayor Donald Hocke (driving), Don Miller, and Charles Falwell. *Courtesy of Harvey Farr*

LEHIGH VALLEY
PENNSYLVANIA

key of the Keystone State

The new $50 million Homer Research Laboratories of Bethlehem Steel Corporation occupy an imposing mountain site in Bethlehem, above Lehigh University campus. Lehigh and Northampton Counties are in view.

Side by side in the heart of downtown Allentown are the just dedicated 8-story Lehigh County Court House and the new Allentown City Hall—a $12 million-plus investment in meaningful urban renewal.

The City of Bethlehem, located in both counties, is building a $6.4 million City Center including a Library financed largely by public and corporate gifts.

The neo-classic Northampton County Court House towers high on a hill in the county seat city of Easton, where the Lehigh and Delaware Rivers come together.

204

Chapter Nine

Center of a Growing Web

Like other cities across the nation, Allentown became involved in urban renewal projects from the early sixties, taking advantage of federal funds earmarked for upgrading American urban centers. In Allentown's case, whole sections of town were torn down, and the residents, including many elderly persons, blacks, and ethnics, were forced to relocate.

Some of the houses that went down in the sixties and seventies were in deplorable condition; others were livable but not worth renovation costs. Still others, insist some Allentonians, would have been treasured historic landmarks if restored. The Nonnemaker house was one such building in the wrong place at the wrong time. At any rate, the value of the urban renewal project continues to be a topic of controversy.

Everyone compelled to leave found it hard, but for Allentonians who had lived in their houses for twenty-five, forty, or even sixty years, it was especially painful. Businesses too had to dig up roots and try to find new, affordable locations. Rentals had tended to be lower in areas marked for renewal than in the rest of the city, so some families and businesses were put to great disadvantage by having to move out, despite federal assistance meant to defray costs. On the other hand, government funding allowed some people to move into sections of town that previously had been closed to them.

The man who served as director of relocation for twenty years, Reverend Horace A. Melton, felt that, all in all, urban renewal was a blessing in disguise:

Playing for the highest stakes, Allentown and other Lehigh Valley cities sported an image of architectural elegance—and corporate and civic expense—to lure major businesses to the area. Allentown's "meaningful urban renewal," spotlighted in this September 1965 advertisement in the *New York Times,* continues in the promise of renovation and renewal in its business district and neighborhoods. *Courtesy of Grace Seibert*

In spite of the fact that there were some houses torn down that should not have been torn down (but they were in the area, you see), when it came to housing, sales or rental, who lived in those houses? The poor, the minorities. The houses perched right on the banks of the river, down on Lawrence Street. The only way you had access to those houses was a metal fire escape to get in and out. There were many other areas with bad housing, and—not that the rent was that cheap—but it was all the housing that was available to minorities. So when urban renewal came along, it was a blessing in disguise because minority persons eventually had access to housing practically anywhere in the city...if they could pay the price. As for the apartment housing, that opened up substantially in proportion to what people could pay. So people got better housing out of the deal. If urban renewal had not come along, private industry would not have, *could* not have rehabilitated all of the necessary housing. Some real estate people contended that we did not need public housing. You would be amazed to know how difficult it was to get public housing in this town. Hanover Acres over here was the first and only one for many, many years. We fought tooth and nail about the time urban renewal was getting off the ground to get some additional public housing, federally financed housing. The real estate board fought it like anything. So finally we got Gross Towers up here. That's housing for the elderly.... The trend now is not for demolition but for rehabilitation.

The trend toward rehabilitation represented a turnaround. Rather than "tear down, build anew," Allentonians began to beautify and modernize existing structures to suit their needs, which proved to be a gratifying, and generally less expensive, alternative. By the mid-1970s, historic districts were designated in the city and strict zoning codes came into effect in an effort to preserve the city's heritage. Businesses became involved in rehabilitating city houses and run-down mills. The Rodales of Rodale Press, for example, renovated three center city houses for their Ann Ar Bookstore, Design Center, and Soup Bowl (a restaurant), and converted a church into the J. I. Rodale Theater, which houses the Pennsylvania Stage Company. On a small scale, professionals such as doctors, dentists, and insurance brokers have set up offices all over town in rowhouses and the old Victorian mansions along west Hamilton Street.

Larger businesses in the retail district of Hamilton have seen many changes from the fifties and into the eighties. Though they had long enjoyed the reputation as the main shopping attraction in the Lehigh Valley,

the coming of the malls in the sixties seriously undermined business. Consumers fell in love with the indoor, weatherless shopping environments with all the new stores, and Hamilton Street retailers found themselves in trouble. Where once a Saturday night on Hamilton was filled with shoppers and activity, suddenly there was only a handful of people. The draw to Whitehall Mall (and later Lehigh Valley Mall, Trexler Mall, and others) gradually put several old Hamilton Street establishments out of business: Zollinger-Harned, Young's, and Kuhns and Shankweiler, for example. Center city was dying, and something had to be done.

As has long been the case in the city, local leaders rallied to back the merchants in town, and a conscious, ongoing program of revitalization was begun. The city built a superstructure of steel and Plexiglas to canopy the sidewalks and crosswalks from Tenth Street to Sixth Street. The sidewalks were remade in patterns of brick and white cement, trees were planted, benches and sculptures installed, and the overall appearance was made "modern." The result was called Hamilton Mall. Down the street on the corner of Fifth Street opposite the post office, the city built a new and modern-looking City Hall, and the county erected an eight-story Lehigh County Court House, which together cost over $12 million.

Efforts to pick up center city and bring back business continue in the eighties. In 1981 the Hilton Hotel came to Allentown at Ninth and Hamilton, designed to attract conventions and serve as headquarters for guests of the large area corporations such as Air Products. Several new restaurants, boutiques, and other service establishments opened on Hamilton Mall, showing a confidence in the city's attraction.

The arrival of the Hilton punctuated what can best be described as a cosmopolitan trend, a trend that has been continuing steadily in Allentown since World War II. Part of the broadened scope is due to the war itself and to other conflicts such as the Korean conflict and Vietnam. As young Allentonians continued to leave to fight in foreign lands and as television became a stronger force, the world at large became part of the local community. The main newspaper, the *Call-Chronicle*, also played an influential role as it switched its focus from local and community events to national coverage.

County executive Dave Bausch observed the trend toward universality and expressed his views:

I think of Air Products as being a major contributor to the cosmopolitan kind of atmosphere, and also the expansion of the Rodale Press and its focus on a different clientele than we're used to having here in the valley. Air Products' Leonard Pool certainly, in himself, was a contributor to a different type of atmosphere. Getting away from the power brokers that were so traditional to the community, like the General [Trexler] and the Youngs. Now, of course, you have the Bermans. They're not native Allentonians, but they're very influential and they brought a different kind of dimension to the city: they're very cosmopolitan in attitude....And in the market area we're very attractive, close to the major centers. We're getting a lot of pressure from the city, from Philadelphia. Residents are moving up, pushing up to Quakertown and up toward us....

I remember when there were cornfields where the mall is. That's just in my lifetime. There were orchards and cornfields surrounding the city of Allentown. That doesn't exist any more. It's lost that smallness. Allentown, while it was a fairly large city, had the impression of being a relatively compact, important city....You seemed to know everybody. Now you go downtown and see people, and you don't know where they came from. That may have been just the perception of a young person, but you felt like you were all part of the community. And now you're a fragment of it.

Allentown's very identity, suggests Bausch, is now unclear. Shopping is no longer what it was as the malls draw customers from throughout the valley. As industry is forced to build facilities outside city limits, owing to lack of land space, Allentonians find themselves relocating beyond the borders.

Said Bausch:

The city is landlocked, basically because they [city government] were annexing so many properties around them and legislation was made that the cities had to stop annexing properties. There's a limit to what they can do. If anything, I see the county as becoming regional government. I'm not saying the people want that, but that's what's happening. I think we're going to see a regional police force, regional fire departments. All those services are going to be on a regional basis in view of becoming one large community.

Ed Miller, former editor of the *Call-Chronicle*, has a similar view:

Allentown is connected to the Lehigh Valley economically, socially, culturally—in every way. City limits are artificial municipal boundaries.

Capital of the Valley

As the borders of the city soften, Allentown's role changes. It is no longer exclusively *the* place to shop, nor is it the big-industry town of years past. Instead, it has come into its own as the center of a growing Lehigh Valley web. As such it is the financial center of the valley. It is also the seat of county government: the Lehigh County Court House, Housing Authority, Historical Society, County Prison, and so forth are all located within Allentown proper. The Allentown Art Museum is the only major museum in the area on a par with those in larger metropolises, and, of course, the Allentown Fair is an event everyone looks forward to. On Super Sunday in September, Allentown is the place where the whole county congregates for an enormous block-party-type street celebration.

As a residential city, Allentown continues to attract immigration. From the mid-sixties on, Hispanic Americans have come into the community, originally seeking work with the textile mills and the orchards. Syrians and Lebanese continue to come, often supported by friends and relatives, some of whom have been established here for sixty years.

In recent decades, Allentown's population has become more transient, and this has caused concern among permanent and old-family residents. A shifting tax base, a stressed economy, and rising crime are also factors that threaten the community's stability. In response, Allentonians have turned attention toward their neighborhoods, and there seems to be renewed interest in maintaining a sense of community for survival as well as for growth. The Old Allentown Preservation Association, largely made up of professionals, and the Old Fairgrounds Neighborhood Association have organized to influence decisions at City Hall. Various cultural associations, such as the Afro-American Center, the Hispanic American Organization, the Arab-American League, and the Jewish Community Center, are community-oriented groups that actively concern themselves with neighborhoods. Encompassing many groups is the Community of Neighborhood Organizations. More informally, residents band together behind causes affecting certain streets or whole neighborhoods.

As a place to live and work, Allentown has much to offer. Becoming cosmopolitan has not necessarily meant isolation or a sense of separateness for city-dwellers. It is still the kind of place where people sit out front and socialize in the warm months and look forward to the new baby on the block. A person considering a move to Allentown might very well hear, "It's a nice place to raise a family." In essence, Allentown is what it always has been, a people's city. Not scintillating, but solid. Its uniqueness lies in its people and its history.

From the Adelaide Mill at lower left to Hess's parking plaza at upper right, the city's varied architecture stretches across this east view from Hamilton to Linden and the Lehigh River to Ninth Street. In the foreground are the PP&L's main power lines. *Photograph by Ken Bloom, 1982*

The city of Allentown is laid out against a backdrop of South Mountain from the vantage point of Whitehall's Lehigh Valley Mall. *Photograph by Ken Bloom, 1982*

Lehigh County's old and new courthouses stand on opposite corners of Fifth and Hamilton. The old building houses the Lehigh County Historical Society. *Photograph by Ken Bloom, 1982*

MacArthur Road in Whitehall is a well-worn path that becomes Seventh Street as it leads into Allentown. At the top of the hill is the Soldiers and Sailors Monument; the smokestack at right belongs to the Lehigh Valley Farms cooperative. *Photograph by Ken Bloom, 1982*

An aerial view from the *Morning Call* helicopter shows the many firemen battling a raging inferno on the upper stories of the Rosa Manufacturing Mill at Tenth and Chestnut streets. Streams of water were also trained on the rooftops of the rowhouses across the street from the factory in an effort to contain the blaze. The mill was ruined, and seven houses were damaged on that balmy April 24, 1982. *Photograph by Joany Carlin; courtesy of* Call-Chronicle newspapers

Along Tilghman Street in the Sixth Ward is one rowhouse with a distinctive onion-dome entrance announcing a Syrian-owned men's clothing store. *Photograph by Ken Bloom, 1981*

The figure of Christ dominates the cityscape overlooking Allentown from the cemetery of St. John the Baptist Slovak Church on Front Street. *Photograph by Ken Bloom, 1982*

Rowhouses and St. Stephen's Lutheran Church on Turner Street in the 1400 block. *Photograph by Ken Bloom, 1982*

211

Waiting for a bus on Hamilton Mall, 1982. *Photograph by Paul Teter*

Shopping with Benny on Hamilton Mall in 1981. *Photograph by Ken Bloom*

Rodney, Kenyon, and Jomo in center city Allentown, 1981. *Photograph by Ken Bloom*

Catherine McQuillan, a warper, inspects many hundreds of silk threads. After 100 years of silk weaving in Allentown, one solitary silk mill survives—the Catoir. *Photograph by Ken Bloom, 1981*

Mayor Joe Daddona (left) and the Hilton's Phil Berman exchange greetings at the mayor's inaugural party, held at the Hilton Hotel in January 1982. *Photograph by Ken Bloom*

The Hispanic American Organization, a self-help agency, has arranged housing, employment, and counseling for Hispanic citizens in the community. Among its many activities and services, acculturation and English-language classes are offered. Taught by Raymond Spencer, this English class represents the mixture of ages and backgrounds of those wishing to "make it" in their new home. *Photograph by Ken Bloom, 1982*

Elliott's Diner

To all appearances Elliott's was just another diner—ham 'n' egg specials, regular customers, and waitresses that heard a lot of stories. But Elliott's Diner had a reputation unmatched by any other eating establishment in town. From 1969, the diner's owner and chief cook, Elliott Holden, fed anyone and everyone. Among Elliott's regulars of doctors and policemen were many of Allentown's street people, the so-called nuisance population that other restaurants tried to avoid, including indigents, former mental patients from the state hospital, and the just plain down-and-out. Many times the Salvation Army sent hungry people ("transits") over to the diner with a slip of paper good for a two-dollar meal. For two dollars you could eat sausage and eggs, home fries, toast, and coffee at Elliott's. The prices were the lowest around, but even so, some could not afford to pay, and so they ate on credit. As long as people paid up every so often, Elliott would keep on filling the plates.

Jean Holden worked at the diner with her father and mother, and she explained how it worked:

> For the whole neighborhood it was a barter system. The tailor up the street did all my dad's clothes and ate there at the diner. The typewriter place next door fixed our adding machines and ate there. The gas station ate lunch there, and then everyone got gas at their place. Everyone just traded off....My dad liked knowing that he could give people credit and they would pay him. He liked the fact that you could still trust people, I think.

Elliott Holden recalled his main customers over time:

> It seemed like over the thirteen years there, we had maybe five different trends in the type of business we got flooded with. When we used to get sales clerks from Zollinger-Harned, that was good going then. That was nice. When I first went to Sixth and Linden, we had an awful lot of drunks because the Caboose [a bar] was going full blast and the Midtown Motel was going full blast and the New Orleans Lounge....It was rough. And we had a lot of business. Then that kind of calmed down, and for awhile we had Jesus freaks. We were loaded with them. They used to have their headquarters down at Sixth and Hickory. Then for a while the bulk of our business came from some kind of government training school—OIC—there at Sixth and Linden where the Midtown Motel was. They would flood in. Then a lot of the business at the end was people from the state hospital. They weren't all that bad.

They were different, but they weren't bad. Sometimes you did have to tell them it was time to leave, or else they would sit there for the whole day....But they were preferable over drunks. I always said happiness is when the waitresses came in the kitchen and said, "Mr. Holden, there's a drunk out front," and when I went out he was smaller than I was.

Changes in the downtown, such as the closing of Zollinger's, and rising costs took their toll. Although he claims he did not get involved with his customers ("If you start talking to them and listening, why you didn't get anything done"), Elliott considered what would become of the people he had been feeding, some of whom were unable to count the money they received from Social Security:

> I thought, My God, what would these people do without me? But I figure there's enough welfare to take care of them somehow.

Ida ("Mom") *Photographs by Jean Holden, 1982*

Waitress Jeri Santos

Gloria

"Rev"

"Rocco"

Lieutenant Dick Flately

Dr. Weaver

Helen Datesman

Count Basie drew a crowd big enough to fill center square in August 1980. The view is on Seventh Street, looking south. *Photograph by Call-Chronicle newspapers; courtesy of Leh's Department Store*

People from all over Lehigh County anticipate Super Sunday, Allentown's big community fair held every September on Hamilton Mall. A wide variety of groups and individuals participate for fun and fund raising, including neighborhood groups, church groups, artists, craftspeople, and local radio stations. On Super Sunday in 1980, Syrian-American men joined hands to dance in front of the Industrial Valley Bank (center), and the mothers of Central Catholic raised funds for the Music Parents Association (bottom).

Two women rested with balloons distributed by the Girl Scouts, and a crowd watched disco dancing as children slept in their parents' arms. A prime attraction that day was the Jaycees' "Khomeini," the target of a dunking contest. *Photographs by Ken Bloom*

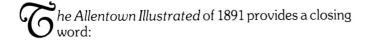
All is quiet on Lawrence Street after a spring snow, 1982. Before urban renewal, the whole area was lined with houses. The highrise in the background behind the Eighth Street Bridge was built to house elderly citizens. *Photograph by Ken Bloom, 1982*

George Weiss presents his retirement photo during an interview in 1981. *Photograph by Ken Bloom*

The Allentown Illustrated of 1891 provides a closing word:

We are so apt to look for beauty only abroad and in the distance, that we fail to see it near at hand and at home. As we glance, then, at the merits of our city, let us realize the fact of what we have, and appreciate the possibilities enfolded therein. Nature has gifted us lavishly; with but little outlay for our numbers and wealth, how much embellishment we might add thereto! Public spirit should be fostered in the artistic direction; it would be an education for us and for those who follow us. Ancient cities prided themselves upon the sacrifices they had made, as communities, to adorn their streets, and squares and groves. Why should not modern cities do so likewise? "A thing of beauty is a joy forever," and a city of beauty need not be any the less, for that reason, a city of thrift, industry, material progress, intellectual strength or social eminence. On the contrary, it is far more likely to become such by harmonious development."

The Little Lehigh wends its way toward Mack Truck, 1982. *Photograph by Ken Bloom*

ACKNOWLEDGMENTS

We are grateful to all of you who gave freely of your time, memories, and photographs. Special credit goes to Takla Gardey for her editorial contributions.

CONSULTANTS

Florence T. Bloom, Ph.D.
Charlene S. Engel, Ph.D.
Wilson F. Engel, Ph.D.

INTERVIEWS

William Albert
Glenn Aranyos and John Havassy
David K. Bausch
Lester Bender
Joseph Bierman, M.D.
Lloyd W. Bowman
Louis Buehler
William Butz
Esther Max Coleman
Jay Birney Crum
    (Bill Fritsch, interviewer)
Ruth Wertman Dannecker
Charles E. Daniels
Frank A. DeChristopher
Anna Ernst
Samuel Fenstermacher, M.D.
William Fiedler and Mrs. Ed Fiedler
Gordon Fister
Grace Frank
J. William Fritsch
Lillian and Frank Gackenbach
William Genszler
Richard Gregg
Edna Hein
Richard Hoffman
Elliott Holden
Jean Holden
Annie and William Jacoby,
    and Mildred Benson
Ruth Junius
Elloda Kemmerer (Judith Harris and
    Becky Carr, interviewers)
Mike Krajsa
Mike Kush
John McClafferty
Bob Manley
Don Marushak
Celia Mellner
Edith Mellner
Rev. Horace A. Melton

Ralph Merkle, M.D.
Ed Miller
Elsie and Harold Moll
Rose Moser
Robert F. Ott
Mrs. Lupe Pearce and Maria Ciuz
Henry Pommer, Ph.D.
Sarah Rinn
Harry Romig
Sally Ruhe Ruhf (Anne Elnitsky and
    Kathy Ellwood, interviewers)
Mildred Trexler Helfrich Schmeyer
Sarah and John Schroeder
John Smicker
Ferdinand Soprano
Patricia Strauss
Liz and Ruth Taylor
Arline and Theodore Trexler
Rev. Francisco Vega
Father Francis Walters
Louis Wasser
George Weiss
Anna Wessner (Eugene Roginsky and
    Jim Morey, interviewers)
Florence Wieland
Rev. Henry Williams
George and Flora Wisser
Sam Wolf
Willard Zimmerman

Credits

Rudy and Rose Ackerman
Air Products and Chemicals Inc.
Allentown Bureau of Inspections
Allentown Bureau of Parks
Allentown Bureau of Police
Allentown Bureau of Recreation
Allentown Hospital
Allentown Public Library
American Association of
    University Women
Rev. Ernest Andrews
Roger and Carol Baldwin
Barnyak Antiques
Edgar Baum, M.D.
Baum School of Art
Terry Benner
Lee Berkley
David Biles
Mrs. Hannelore Blew
Beth Bloom
Linda Bowers
Bob Boyle
Bradley Pulverizer, Inc.
Arthur Bransky
Ray Brennen
Ray and Betty Brong
Steve Brosky
Monica and A. Newton Bugbee
Burkholder Funeral Home

Raymond Butz
Call-Chronicle newspapers
Greta Campbell
Canal Museum
Louis and Martha Capwell
Martha Capwell
Catoir Silk Company
Cedar Crest College
Jeffrey Chambers
Sam Clarke
Mayor Joseph Daddona
Ruth D'Aleo
Henry "Hank" Dannecker
Dan's Camera City
Diocese of Allentown
Lois Doncevic
Dorney Park
Ed Emig
Tracy Ernst
Annie Everett
Tom Everett
Harvey Farr
Lona Farr
Farr Shoes
George Feldman
Frank Fischl
Brian and Rochelle Freedman
Lillian and Frank Gackenbach
Anthony Gardeno
Marian Gehringer
Diana Gottshall
Marge Grabias
Ray Hefflefinger
Mahlon Hellerich, Ph.D.
Hess's Department Store
Charles Hoch
Aral and Naomi Hollenbach
Jewish Community Center
Jim Kelly
Karl Kercher
Charles Kiernan
Marsha Kleedorfer
Mrs. Ethel Kramlick
Rev. Guy Kratzer
Arlene Lakits
Debbie Laubach
Robert H. A. Laudenslager
Sylvia Lawler
David Leh
Leh's Department Store
Lehigh County Historical Society
Liberty Bell Shrine
Jeanette Ludwig
Brother James McCabe
Janice H. McElroy, Ph.D.
Mack Trucks Inc.
Mrs. William F. Mealey
George Meiser
Jane Michael
Larry Miley
Terry Miller
Harold and Rosanne Millman

Moravian College
Vivian Nicholl
Robert S. Ott
Emrika Padus and Tom Herzer
Richard Peifly
Brenda Peluso
Pennsylvania Power and Light
Cathy Perlmutter
Doug Peters
Pollyanna Peters
Phoebe-Devitt Home
Joe Pobereskin
Jackie Poe
Railroads to Yesterday
Paul Rauch
Rebco Kwik Print
William B. Restmeyer
Robin Miller Filmmaker
Anna Rodale
Lillian Rodberg
Bruce Romig
Judd Roth
Marguerite Kehm Sandt
Barbara Satterlee
Polli Sawruk
Ann Scarloss
Grace Seibert
Patty Seip
Althea Sherer
Mrs. Clarence Siegfried
Watson and Vivian Skinner
Smith and Peifly, Inc.
Raymond E. Spencer
Monsignor Thompson
Betty and Kyle Traylor
Twin County Cable TV
Laura Tylersmith
Union Baptist Church
John Vidoni
WFMZ Television
Ben Walbert
Fred Walbert
Kathryn Walton
Bill Waschitsch
Richard Weaver
Susan Weaver
Jerry Weber
Mae Weida
Alice Wick
Carol Wickkiser
Robert Wieland
Joel Wiener
Rev. Henry Williams
Bob Wittman
Dr. and Mrs. Charles Wolbers
Tomas Wolff
Polly Wood
Dolly and George Yanolko
Jerry Yoder
Mrs. John Zettlemoyer
Zion Reformed United Church
    of Christ

Mayors of the City of Allentown

Bibliography

Allentown Illustrated. Allentown: H. R. Page & Co., 1891.

Boyer, Melville J., ed. *Proceedings of the Lehigh County Historical Society,* vol. 22. Allentown: Lehigh County Historical Society, 1958.

Burton, Roy E., Jr. *Allentown Bicentennial 1762-1962, Lehigh County Sesquicentennial 1812-1962.* Allentown: author, 1962.

Evening Chronicle: 100-Year Anniversary Issue, March 7, 1970.

Ewing, Gretchen. "General Harry Trexler: Lehigh Valley Remembers Its Most Famous Leader." *Morning Call,* May 8, 1981.

Fink, Leo Gregory. *Memoirs of General Harry Clay Trexler.* New York: Paulist Press, 1935.

Fritsch, J. Warren. "In the Beginning: Spotlights on the Early Schooldays in Allentown." Unpublished text.

Gobron, L. C., comp. *Allentown 1916: Souvenir of Allentown.* Allentown: author, July, 1916.

Greenberg, William T., Jr., and Kramer, Frederick A., with Gleichmann, Theodore F., Jr. *The Handsomest Trains in the World: Passenger Service on the Lehigh Valley Railroad.* New York: Quadrant Press, 1978.

Hellerich, Mahlon H., ed. *Lehigh Heritage: 75th Anniversary Edition, Proceedings of the Lehigh County Historical Society,* vol. 33. Allentown: Lehigh County Historical Society, 1979.

_____. *Proceedings of the Lehigh County Historical Society,* vol. 34. Allentown: Lehigh County Historical Society, 1980.

1918-1968: 50 Years, Jewish Community Center. Allentown: Jewish Community Center, 1968.

Koons' Illustrated History of the Lehigh Valley. Catasauqua, Pa.: Koons, Albert A.

Kehm, Robert J. "This Is My Life: 1879-1950." Unpublished text.

Kulp, Randolph L., ed. *History of Lehigh Valley Transit Company.* Allentown: Lehigh Valley Chapter, National Railway Historical Society, 1966.

_____. *Railroads in the Lehigh River Valley.* Allentown: Lehigh Valley Chapter, National Railway Historical Society, 1962.

Old Allentown Houses: Design Guidelines for an Historic District. Allentown: Old Allentown Preservation Association, Inc. 1979.

Park Development in Allentown: 1904-1979. Allentown: City of Allentown Bureau of Parks, November 9, 1979.

Roberts, Charles Rhoads, et. al. *History of Lehigh County, Pennsylvania: And a Genealogical and Biographical Record of Its Families,* vols. I, II and III. Allentown: Lehigh Valley Publishing Company, Ltd., 1914.

Sipple, Simon. *History of Zion Reformed Church, Allentown, Pennsylvania: 1762-1937.* Allentown: Press of Berkemeyer-Keck Co., 1937.

The Standard Business and Mailing Guide of Country, Town and City: Lehigh and Northampton County Journal Including the Bethlehems (Pennsylvania). Kutztown, Pa.: Wm. S. Rhode & Co., 1911.

Trexler, LeRoy D., comp. *Historic Allentown.* Allentown: Trexler Funeral Homes.

Trexler, Mildred Rowe, ed. *Proceedings of the Lehigh Country Historical Society,* vol. 28. Allentown: Lehigh County Historical Society, 1970.

Whelan, Frank. "The 8th Street Bridge: A Steel and Concrete Monument to a Turn-of-the-Century Vision." *Morning Call,* August 17, 1981.

Index